JOURNEY OF FAITH

JOURNEY
OF
FAITH

BEN C. DOUGLAS

ELDERBERRY PRESS
OAKLAND

ELDERBERRY PRESS, LLC

1720 Old Homestead Drive, Second floor
Oakland, Oregon 97462—9506.
E-MAIL: editor@elderberrypress.com
www.elderberrypress.com
TEL/FAX: 541.459.6043

All Elderberry books are available from your favorite bookstore, amazon.com, or from our 24 hour order line: (800)431-1579

Library of Congress Control Number: 2003108799
Publisher's Catalog-in-Publication Data
Journey Of Faith/Ben C. Douglas
ISBN 1-930859-62-7
1. Memoir.
2. Restaurants.
3. Teaching.
4. America.
5. New Jersey.
I. Title

This book was written, printed, and bound in the United States of America.

ACKNOWLEDGEMENTS

I am in debt to the following friends who spent many hours on their computers in preparing the manuscript for printing. Grete James, Derek Parish, Billie Downs and Chris Flynn provided excellent work. Hank Guyer must be commended for his proofreading.

Finally, I must extend thanks to my executive editor, David St. John. Many great suggestions he made were outstanding. I've made another new friend. Anything that makes the book good is because of these friends who made sure it would be.

Dedicated to

MAY HERR   JAY HERR

Jay was the compassionate husband,
May the loving wife;
Together they were bonded,
Both had a wonderful life.

During the great depression,
With food, gifts, clothing and toys;
Each made a lasting impression,
On the Johnson girls and boy.

First Jay met his Maker,
Floated away at too young an age;
May followed soon thereafter,
God turned the final page.

PROLOGUE

Snow is softly falling as the Johnsons return home on a cold winter day in early January, 1919. Matilda Johnson's daughter and three sons have been to Evergreen Cemetery where she was entombed in the family plot.

• • •

All the children had been born and reared in the old weather-beaten, two-story house. It was well situated at the top of Park Street in Washington Boro. From the front porch, you could look down and see the Pennsylvania Railroad track running parallel to the mighty Susquehanna River. During the summer, Matilda had often sat upon her old fashioned oak rocker, watching the trains lumbering by, along side the slow moving river.

• • •

Martha and her brothers took chairs around the kitchen table. As the only sister, Martha took her mother's place at the head. About five feet tall, she was dressed all in black. With her glasses loosely attached to her nose, she looked like a perched cat, ready to make a fast move. To Martha's left, John, one of the twins, was casually smoking a black stogie. Not much taller than his sister, his face was heavily crinkled. Dressed in a long-sleeved shirt and black pants and shoes, he looked like a banty rooster about to cackle. Directly across from John, was his twin, Larry. He was definitely identical in height, weight, and general appearance. Facing his sister, Sam was seated between his twin brothers. Since he was a blacksmith, pounding an anvil all day, his arms were muscular and his hands were hardened.

With an all black enrobement, he could have simulated a minister. Martha gave each of her brothers a sheet of paper and suggested they list whatever items they would each like to have. All four headed their list with their mother's rocker. Martha claimed her mother promised it to her. All the brothers chimed in and got very vociferous. Rash accusations were made. The dialogue became over-heated,

After fighting for an hour, John huffed and puffed his way out. He told them he would never talk to any of them again. Larry continued the acrimonious debate and finally stormed out of the door, saying he was finished with all of them. Meanwhile, Sam who had been rather quiet, angrily took a walk, berating everyone for being so stubborn. Martha was left alone to settle the small estate. She wound up with the chair. For the remainder of their lives, the family was split. Sam talked to Larry, but never contacted John. John and Larry, the twins, never bothered each other again. However, all of the brothers were on good terms with Martha.

• • •

Bob, the leading character in 'Journey of Faith', was only a year old at the time of the blow up in the Johnson family.

With his mother's help, he was able to meet and talk with his aunt and twin uncles. All his life he was greatly troubled with the vindictiveness of everyone involved. It taught him a great lesson. He always tried to keep his temper in check and meet people on an even playing field.

Chapter One

The Early Years

On March 10, 1918, a roaring blizzard had inundated Marietta, a small town beside the Susquehanna River. Drifts almost six feet high and a temperature of five below zero, left the house looking like a gigantic snowball. Inside the house on East Market Street, Sarah the midwife was preparing for the birth of Bessie's baby. Towels, sheets and buckets of hot water were carried to the second floor. Meanwhile, seventeen year old Dorothy and John who was now six, were quietly working on their school assignments. An old-fashioned coal stove gave off heat that warmed the kitchen and went upstairs through a vent in the ceiling. Sitting on a rocking chair, Sam Johnson was nonchalantly smoking a stogie and perusing the local paper. After all, a new child is old hat for him. Suddenly a tremendous blast of freezing snow batters the windows. At the same time, a loud wail is heard. Bob, the first born of Bessie and Sam, has been ushered into a world where nations are fighting for survival. Definitely a night that will be long remembered.

• • •

Sam's first wife, Belinda, passed away in 1912. Their marriage was blessed with four children. Two girls, Jane and Francine, and Victor were already married. Dorothy, the youngest, was still with her father. Bessie had only been married two years when Frank died, leaving her with Frank's son. Several years passed and Bessie and Sam were married. Both agreed to take care of the son and daughter from their first marriages.

• • •

Two years after Bob's birth, Bessie and Sam were engaged in almost continuous explosive discussion. Dorothy had flown the coop and was living alone. John was often the target of Sam's pungent remarks. It was a problem that stayed on the hot burner for quite a spell.

• • •

Bob, who seemed to feel the tension between his parents, loved his big brother. He acted as a buffer between John and Sam. It bothered him when Sam would reproach John. Once, when John asked for bread, Sam snarled, "Give him the whole loaf". Bob cringed. From that day forward, he always made sure that John got something to eat. He passed the dishes to John before he ate anything. On his tenth birthday, Bob resolved to wait until he was older and then he was going to tan his father's hide.

• • •

Bob never forgot what John did at Christmas. Sam had given him an extra dollar. His brother bought four gifts, spending twenty cents for each one. He gave a gift to Sam, Bessie, Eloise and Bob. That left him with twenty cents for himself.

• • •

Bob was quite a handful for the family. Quite often his dad would threaten him. "Don't you ever do that again or I'll blister your backside." Bob never paid any attention. He knew his dad just liked to bark at him.

• • •

Running down Market Street were trolley tracks. Every hour the trolley passed the house. Whenever the motorman clanged the bell, Bob jumped up and down and ran after it hollering at the top of his lungs. Bessie got fed up with his shenanigans. She solved this problem by tying a rope around him and held Bob on the sidewalk.

• • •

Bessie always explained that Bob should never play with matches. One day he found a pack of cigarettes. He and his friend Jake climbed to the top of the lumber shed which was full of wooden shingles. Having appropriated a box of matches from the kitchen, they lit one. It fell to the ground. So they lit a second one. It also fell through the woodpile.

Suddenly, Bob remembered what his mother had warned him about matches. So, the two boys spent the next hour looking for the matches they had dropped. This incident stayed in his mind for years. He never lit another match or tried to smoke until he was twenty-five. Bessie was never told.

• • •

One night Sam returned from his club considerably under the weather. Since he rarely drank any liquor, he was definitely out of this world. Bob, who was in the bedroom at the top of the stairs, heard the loud singing and heard his mother say.

"You're a damn fool Sam, shut your big mouth, you'll wake up Bob." Since he was already awake, Bob sat up in bed and watched his father stagger into his bedroom. Shaking his head from side to side, he said, "Dad, you could have used the money on something else".

• • •

Bob's sister, Eloise was born when he was twenty months old. He was almost eight when his youngest sister Jennifer came into the world.

• • •

Sam had been employed at Baker Quarry in Bainbridge as a blacksmith. He used to sharpen drills used in drilling holes in large rocks. After placing dynamite in the hole, a fuse was lit and the rock was broken into smaller units. Placed in a large crusher, the stone was split into fine stone used on highways.

• • •

After Sam lost his job, he moved the family to Stackstown which is near Bainbridge. For three years, Sam became a farmer, working on the half-shares.

Raising cigar tobacco, provided the most money. In addition, wheat, corn and barley were grown.

During the late spring, the tobacco plants were carefully planted. Like a new born baby, the tobacco plants needed constant care. The ground was cultivated numerous times. Walking through the rows of tobacco, with a can of gasoline, Sam and John would shake the tobacco bugs into the can. If they were not removed, the tobacco leaf would have numerous holes and the crop could lose most of its cash value.

In the fall the crops were harvested and placed in the barn. The tobacco was cut and put on a lath and carried to the tobacco barn. There it was left to dry.

About November, the tobacco was taken to the cellar; where the leaves were removed from the stalk. Next, the leaves were sorted according to size. Made into bundles and then placed in bales they were stored in the shed until a tobacco buyer arrived. With an agreed upon price per pound, the entire crop would be hauled away, and the money received would be divided into a share for the farmer and a share for the owner of the farm.

• • •

While living on the farm, Bob managed to keep everyone on their toes. One day he wandered into the wheat field. Since the wheat was taller than he was, he somehow got lost. It started to get dark. Everyone looked for him. When they finally located him in the middle of the field, he was sleeping on the ground.

• • •

Right next to the farm that Sam was farming was a two-story brick schoolhouse. Whenever the children were out at recess, or at lunch time, Bob would be at the fence looking at them playing. He begged his mother to let him go to school. He was several months younger than he should have been. However, the teacher agreed to take him anyhow. Bob really loved school and would read all the time.

• • •

Whenever the tobacco crop was cut down, the farmers always left a few of the best plants to develop seed for the next years crop. Bob and his friend from the next farm, decided that Sam had forgotten a few plants. So the two boys cut them down and brought them into the tobacco shed. They meant well, but it was one of the times that Sam almost lost his cool. However, after the boys explained that they were only trying to help, Sam passed it off, even laughing when he told Eloise later.

• • •

One of the farmers close by Sam's farm was worth several hundred thousand dollars. He got to talking to Sam about insurance. When he found out Sam had a policy for five thousand dollars, he encouraged Sam to cash it in. Sam listened. Several years later when he died the family was left with only two hundred dollars to bury him. The funeral cost one hundred and forty dollars, so they had sixty dollars left.

Several years later, the gentleman who told Sam to cash in his policy, died. He left an insurance policy worth two hundred thousand dollars. Bob remembered and later always provided enough protection for his own family.

• • •

After several years on the farm, Sam was offered a position as a blacksmith in a quarry. Omrod, a small community about five miles from the city of Allentown. They stayed at Egypt and moved three times during four years.

• • •

Bob enjoyed school at all times. However, while in the fifth grade he ran into a very inflexible teacher, called Miss Hooker. One day, while in class, Bob was caught talking. Called to the front of the class, he was beaten for quite a spell with a big wooden paddle. Bob decided that he was not going to cry. At recess time, Bob's friends asked if it hurt. For one of the times in his life, Bob lied. After returning to class, after recess, one of his friends (?) raised his hand and told Miss Hooker, "Bob said the paddling didn't hurt."

Miss Hooker's face turned red. She called Bob to the front and proceeded to whale him until she couldn't whip him anymore. However, Bob never cried once.

Bob's mother never heard about the paddling until the next year. She heard the boys talking. She asked Bob, "Why didn't you tell me about the licking?"

"If I had said anything you would have burnt my britches."

• • •

During summer vacation, Bob went off to the quarry where his father worked. A special time was always when the men dynamited a large section of the limestone quarry causing a mountain of rock to splinter off and roll to the ground.

Many times he used to crawl around the rock. Once when his dad worked in a quarry near Allentown, he decided to climb down the face of the rock. He had done this many times, but this time was different. Reaching the halfway point, he discovered there was no way to get down to the bottom. Then he looked up and forgot how he had climbed so far. For about two hours, he panicked.

Finally he managed courageously to climb back up. Knowing how Bessie would react if he told her about the climb, he kept it quiet. Years later he explained what happened to his mother.

• • •

Bob played with some of the boys whose parents had come to America from Hungary, Romania, Czechoslovakia, Austria, and other Eastern European countries. On the Fourth of July, Bob had some fire crackers, so they all went back in the alley and got an old tin can. Taking the fire crackers apart, they put the powder into the can.

Several times they attempted to light the powder. No result. Finally, Bob got real close, set the match and BOOM! The powder burnt his hair and face.

He was fortunate that his eyes were not affected.

• • •

Often Bob went along with his friends to an old quarry hole filled with water. It was one hundred feet deep. They dove into the water and swam around. At times Bob was urged to try it out, even though he could not swim. Finally, after they showed him what to do and promised to help him, he entered the water. He paddled out a few feet at a time. After several sessions he was confident he could swim and often joined them. Needless to say, Bessie never knew about it until years later.

• • •

Once a week, from June to September, Bob went along to help a grocer, who delivered food to homes of men, working in the cement mills. All of them lived in company homes and most of the families barely survived. His eyes opened wide when he carried groceries into the homes. Most of the homes had no rugs or covering on the floor and very little furniture.

Bob, seeing the conditions in which the families lived, told Bessie how lucky they were to have enough to eat.

• • •

A year later Sam lost his job. Bessie worked sixty hours in a sweat shop. She walked three miles to work, put in twelve hours and then walked three miles home for twelve dollars a week.

Sam attempted to cook. Frankly he was at a complete loss. For a whole year they survived on potatoes and bread. They had fifteen bushels of potatoes in the cellar. Once a week, they bought left over bread from the factory. However all managed to weather the storm.

Everything Sam and Bessie had saved was gone. Even the home in Marietta was sold.

• • •

Every day Bob went to Whitehall Township on a trolley car. At the time he was in the seventh grade.

Bessie gave her son fifteen cents to buy his lunch. He could get a hot-dog, milk and dessert. However, he only used the money he received one week. Without telling anyone, he saved the money during the winter, and when the family moved back to Marietta, he gave his mother all the money in his can. When asked why he didn't spend it, "Well mom, I knew you needed the money so I saved it".

His mother realized why Bob had always rushed to the kitchen and ate some bread when he returned in the afternoon.

• • •

While the family lived in Egypt, Sam took the family back to Lancaster every month. Bessie had to see Dr. John who was treating her for cancer.

Everyone looked forward to staying at Grammy Meister's house. They all especially enjoyed her home-made bread and pies. Even though she had a serious heart problem, she never complained.

Bob really loved his Grandmother and was always helping her with many chores.

Grandpa Meister was a typical Prussian. He would have made a good dictator. Bob never pleased him. In fact, he seemed to take great pleasure in hollering at Bob.

"Don't touch that hammer. Leave that saw alone. Get out of my shed."

Whenever he could, Bob would avoid his grandfather. He knew he was always in the dog house. It affected him for many years.

• • •

On Sundays, Sam took Bessie and Bob's two sisters for a ride in the Old Tin Lizzie. No one could figure out why Bob never wanted to go.

As soon as the family left, Bob gathered up all the books that he had brought home, and returned them to his neighbors. He would select four or five new books and start reading. When he heard the car returning he'd hide the books under the bed or chiffonier. Very nonchalantly opening the back door, he'd ask them if they had a pleasant trip.

• • •

Horatio Alger books were especially popular during the Depression. Every book followed the same basic theme. Starting out as poor children, working hard, making good and ending up rich and famous. Bob visualized his life overcoming all obstacles and finishing up as a great business man.

• • •

Sam and Bessie never realized that Bob was very nearsighted. While going to school, he always had to sit at the front of the class so that he could see any writing on the blackboard. Knowing that his parents had very little money, he never divulged his secret.

Finally his teacher realized that he had a problem and arranged an eye exam for him. After the exam she provided him with glasses. Bob felt that he was entering a new world. Never again, during his lifetime, was he without his spectacles.

• • •

Bessie and Sam were too proud to ask for any help. When they prepared to move back to Lancaster County, some of the neighbors talked to Bessie. They had heard they were having a tough time. All of them said they would have helped us, if they had known.

It made us all feel real good to know how much people cared.

Chapter Two

High School Days

Early in September, Bob started in the Eighth Grade. Miss Hinkle, a wonderful spinster lady was the class teacher. On the first day, she outlined what she expected the class to accomplish throughout the school year.

In addition, she explained that at the end of the school year, she would take the class to the Philadelphia Zoo. However, there were a number of conditions that must be met. First and foremost, the class was expected to get good passing grades.

Each week, for thirty weeks, each student was required to bring five cents to help pay the expenses for the trip. Bob, who had never been to a big city, eagerly awaited the great event. At last the big day arrived. All of the classmates met in front of the school at 6:30 am. Everyone carried a box lunch and a few fortunate persons had also been given fifty cents or a dollar to spend. At last a large truck arrived. It was equipped with hard wooden benches. In a few minutes, everyone was seated and the trip began very smoothly.

Excitement was very high since only three members of the class had ever been to the zoo. Taking US Route 30, the driver proceeded slowly towards Philly. Members of the class were either talking quietly or observing the scenery.

Reaching the zoo, the class left the truck with their lunch pails. Miss Hinkle suggested they should stay close together. In case anyone became separated, they were to stop and wait for her. Most of the girls were intrigued with the small monkeys and the many beautiful birds. The boys were awed by the lions, tigers and elephants.

At noon time, everyone gathered around picnic tables and enjoyed eating and resting for a short time. As an extra bonus, the class was provided with ice cream cones. After lunch the class observed bears, giraffes, rhinos. leopards and various other animals.

Finally, at 4:30 p.m., they started on the journey home. Some class members talked about the animals that interested them and others sang a few school songs. Reaching home, all were talking about the great time that they enjoyed. Before dispersing, each student expressed their appreciation to Miss Hinkle.

• • •

During the summer, Sam was employed in a quarry in Havre de Grace, Maryland. However, he was only able to get home once a month.

Meanwhile, Bob enjoyed himself working with his neighbors and helping out with various odd jobs. He was especially very helpful with the elderly ladies. He often stopped in to see how he could help. He would enjoy hearing odd stories about their problems.

Before leaving, a glass of cookies and milk were provided.

• • •

After the summer season passed, Bob entered High School as a freshman. He weathered the three month hazing period and plunged into life - full steam ahead.

Actually, he enjoyed school at all times. None of the subjects gave him any trouble. History was his favorite. As an elective, he chose French 1.

Miss Stimson, who taught French, was a new teacher. Naturally, some the mavericks gave her a hard time. One day, Paul Johnson brought a pair of handcuffs along. Seeing one of his pals with his hands behind his back, Paul proceeded to handcuff him to his chair. Adding insult to injury, the keys were thrown out of the window.

Just then, Miss Stimson called on Henry Stern to stand up and read a paragraph in the French book. Henry insisted that he couldn't stand up. Finally, in desperation, he stood up. Everyone in the class heehawed. Miss Stimson charged out of the room and returned with the principal. Very quietly he informed the class to meet him after school for a one hour detention.

• • •

Although Bob talked to all the girls in school, he never asked them for a date.

Never having any spare change, he couldn't very well ask them out. Acting very shy, he covered himself.

Basketball season started in October. Naturally, he was one of the first to sign up. Unfortunately, he had to remove his glasses. No matter what he did, he never seemed to see the ball coming. As a result, it often hit his body and fell to the floor. Many games he never played for even a minute. In order to see all the games at home and away, he took over as team manager. It meant that he was responsible for all balls and equipment. During home games, he collected all tickets and money as the spectators entered the gym. One night he turned up 15 cents short. Principal Henson, a stickler for the last penny, kept Bob for over an hour until the money was located.

● ● ●

Around November, Bob's father returned home. Once again he had been laid off.

Finally, in the middle of November, Sam was employed in a tobacco warehouse. Steam was utilized to keep the tobacco moist. It was too much for Sam. He contracted pneumonia. Over the past year, he had often skipped meals and was suffering from malnutrition. His condition deteriorated.

One morning in the first week of March '32, his physician, Dr. John Simon's came to the house at 6:00 a. m. At 12:30 he returned to check on his patient. Once again at 5:30 p.m. he came back and said that he would return late. He made his last visit at 1:00 a.m. Finally at 1:30, Dr. John got down on his knees and prayed for Sam. In five minutes, Sam had passed on to a better world.

Eloise was with her father and Dr. John. Bessie and Bob were downstairs.

Jennifer, the youngest was sleeping. She had a very hard time accepting Sam's death. Sam was laid out in the parlor. Jennifer never went in the parlor again.

• • •

Sam's friends came from miles around to attend the services. Bob counted fifty cars that followed the hearse to the cemetery. He had never realized how many friends his father had known.

After paying for the funeral, Bessie had fifty six dollars left. She sold the old Studebaker for one hundred twenty-five dollars. That was all they had to meet expenses.

• • •

One week after Sam's funeral, Uncle John who had not spoken to Sam or his twin brother for years, came to the house bringing some food and clothes for Eloise, Jennifer and Bob. He told Bessie that he didn't attend the funeral because he didn't want to be a hypocrite. Over the next few years he continued to visit every few weeks.

• • •

Bessie's first husband Frank had died when John, his son was only a year old.

Frank's sister and her husband Jay Herr, came to see them on Easter Sunday after the funeral. May knew that Bessie had taken good care of Frank. She came to see how she could help. Since it was Easter, they had brought some Easter candy and a few trinkets for all of the family.

• • •

During the next three years, they came almost every month, bringing food and gifts. Their compassion and concern for the family impressed Bob. Throughout his life, he tried to emulate Jay. Whenever he met someone in need, he tried to give them support.

Several times they were invited to their home for a visit. On one visit, Jay took Bob out to a local tennis court. Several times when talking about tennis, Bob had said that it was a sissy game. Jay handed him a tennis racket and they started to hit the ball back and forth. Suddenly, Jay started to increase the tempo, hitting the ball everywhere on the court but where Bob stood. After about twenty minutes. Jay stopped the slaughter. Another valuable lesson for Bob. From that day forward, he attempted to think before he uttered any foolish ideas.

• • •

About a year before Sam died, Bob stayed at Grandma Meister's home every night. He slept on the second floor, and whenever he heard Grandpa yelling at Grandma to get up and make him a cup of coffee, he'd hurry down and do it himself. He knew she suffered from a serious heart condition. Once again, he served as a buffer between two people that he loved.

• • •

Quite often, Bob and his Grandparents played pinochle. Grandpa was a prime example of a poor loser. Often he would speak harshly to his wife. Bob managed to level the playing field. In pinochle, the object of the game is to attempt to get the most points. Aces, Kings and tens were counted as a single point. Grandpa didn't win too often, Bob would throw pointers on his Grandma's tricks and non-pointers on his Grandfather's. As a result, Grandma would win the game. If she won two games, all the cards would be thrown on the floor. Bob would quickly pick them up. Even though he knew he was cheating, he enjoyed watching the child-like tantrums. It gave him immense satisfaction to protect Grandma.

Bob was once stopped by a middle-aged man who was dressed rather slovenly. He appealed for funds and said that he hadn't eaten for two days. Taking a quarter, the only money that he had, Bob gave it to the man. However, something about the man didn't ring true, so he decided to follow him. Walking to Front Street, he entered a bar. With the door open, Bob watched the individual consume five glasses of beer. Never afterwards would he give money to anyone. If they wanted food or a carfare, Bob would offer to go with them and pay for it. Needless to say most of them walked away.

• • •

Marietta, with a population of almost 2,000 had two main thoroughfares, Market Street and Front street. As in most small communities, there were a few well-known characters.

One was Tillie, who was a bag lady. All the children thought that she was a witch. Actually, she lived alone and never bothered anybody. Bob managed to become friendly with her and couldn't understand the treatment that she received. Her house was set back close to an alley and her grass plot was covered with various nicknacks that she had collected over the years. She often traded or sold her little treasures.

• • •

The town's local undertaker was so bad that his son left him and set up his own business. Jake would visit those individuals who were very sick, with little hope of recovery. He always brought with him a bouquet of flowers. Before leaving, he often took out a tape measure and figured out what size coffin would be needed. You might say that he came prepared.

• • •

One of the towns richest individuals was married to a woman of vile temper and speech. She made her daughter-in-law's life a real hell on earth. Her son was so much under her thumb, that he never really acted like a real husband.

• • •

Other individuals were universally admired. Birdie, the local postman, was always cheerful and helped others. This, in spite of the fact that he had intestinal problems all his life.

Mary was a wonderful Sunday School teacher. She always had a large class. At Christmas time, she gave out Hulbert's Story of the Bible to all those who had a perfect attendance for the year.

• • •

Grandma Meister had a beautiful cherry tree that was loaded with big black cherries. Bob usually picked them on half shares, half for Grandma and half for himself. Placing a ladder against the tree, he would climb almost to the top. Setting on a thick branch, he would first start eating until his stomach was full. Robins provided him with a little competition. Bob always left some cherries on each branch so that the birds enjoyed themselves. After he picked twenty quarts, he stopped and gave his Grandmother ten quarts which she canned for the winter. Bob sold his cherries for 5 cents a quart. Besides making a few pennies, he had thoroughly enjoyed his favorite fruit.

• • •

Six months after his father's death, Bob met a businessman who sold dairy products for a big milk company in Lancaster. He agreed to sell cottage cheese, heavy cream and especially a well-known butter that was sold in the local store. Part of the agreement was that Bob had to sell the butter at the same price as the local grocery. Starting with about fifteen pounds of butter, he gradually built up his route. Adding customers each week until he was selling ninety pounds of butter, four quarts of heavy cream, and fifteen packages of cottage cheese. All through high school, he continued selling the dairy products. Quite often, in order to meet the local store price he would only make one or two cents per pound. Jerry, the business representative for the dairy, promised to help financially when Bob enrolled at Millersdale State Teachers College.

• • •

Bessie made old fashion stick candy. Eloise and Jennifer often sold 200 or 300 sticks a week for one cent a piece. Bob sold apples for a neighbor lady for few extra pennies. Milk was purchased by the gallon for five cents a quart. Leaving it stand overnight, heavy cream collected on the top, which was used in making toppings for Jello pudding and ice cream.

• • •

Twice Bob attempted to work on a farm. Starting at 6:00 a.m. until 8:00 p.m. he moved the bales of straw into a huge pile that reached twenty feet in height. At lunch time, thinking he might get more money he went home and ate. However, at 6:00 p.m. he ate at the farm. When they finally finished up for the day, the farmer started paying all the helpers. Some received three or four dollars, others two dollars. All were paid except Bob. He approached the farmer and said that he wanted his pay. Reaching into his pocket, he generously gave Bob thirty five cents. Bob felt like throwing it at him. But then he decided he'd keep it. He told Bessie he wasn't going to help do anymore threshing on the farm again.

• • •

Several months later, another farmer, who sold vegetables, asked Bob to help him out. Against his better judgement, he agreed. After walking three miles, he reached the farm. He was to handle 3 horses hitched to a cultivator and loosen the dirt in the corn field. Even though he was told how to handle the team of horses, he was a complete disaster, He made only one run about a mile long. Instead of cultivating, he proceeded to pull the young plants out of the ground. Following him the poor farmer was busily replanting what had been torn up. When he finally reached the cultivator, Bob and the farmer mutually agreed that as a cultivator he was a bust, so he returned home. Telling Bessie he would never work on a farm again, he certainly kept that promise.

• • •

Three of Bob's classmates often visited at his home or theirs. Clete was 6 foot 2 inches, a bean pole who was a sub on the basketball team. Denny, was about 5 foot 10 inches, was always the live wire in any meeting. His loud guffaw was so contagious everyone couldn't help laughing. Charles, who was born blind in one eye, was a happy-go-lucky type. He also became a first class artist. Usually, a game of Pinochle was played. Each game was spirited. At the end of the games, each would receive a piece of lemon meringue pie and tea or coffee.

• • •

Any money that Bob was able to make was immediately

turned over to his mother.

With the depression in full swing, the family along with thousands of others managed to survive.

With money in such short supply, Bob rarely got to the movies. Once in a while, someone would go on a pass to the movies. Since it was good for two admissions, Bob's friend in the box office would call him and thus he got a ticket for a nickel instead of a quarter.

• • •

During his high school years, Bob was often in a spirited competition with Fran Shelby. No matter how much he tried he usually came in second. She was the Valedictorian while Bob gave the Salutatory address.

For four years, the class of 1935 with 19 members had been engaged in raising money by giving plays, selling candy and cookies and other projects. Enough money was raised to pay all expenses for three days and two nights in Washington, DC. Mount Vernon was visited; A White House tour was taken; visiting the Capitol building, they watched Congress in action; climbed the Washington monument; visited the Lincoln and Jefferson Memorials; saw the Library of Congress; the Arlington National Cemetery and other points of interest.

On the first night in Washington the class started walking back to the Roosevelt hotel at about 7. Bob decided to stay out and really see Washington at night. He quietly left the class and started his own private tour. Having perused many pamphlets about Washington, prior to the trip, he covered Pennsylvania and Constitution Avenues looking at all the important buildings and places.

Reaching the hotel at 12:30, Bob was hit with lots of questions.

"Where did you go?"

"Were you lost?"

"When did you leave the class?"

"What did you do for five hours?"

The teacher in charge castigated him quite forcefully. He was informed that he would be kept in his room if he didn't follow instructions. Really, Bob felt very good that he had seen all the sights. So he promised to stay close to his classmates for the next two days.

Returning to Marietta, everyone looked forward to the summer. Some of the class prepared for college, while others took positions in the community and other towns. Four years of high school had prepared them for life's next step. It was time to move forward.

Chapter Three

College

Bob had scheduled a meeting in Lancaster to meet Jerry, the business man who had promised to provide him with tuition for Millersville State Teacher"s College. He had worked for Jerry for over 3 years.

Reaching Lancaster, Bob met Jerry in front of the Hamilton Watch Company. After exchanging greetings, Bob asked him how business was developing.

"I'm afraid I have bad news for you. Business is very poor. I am sorry, but I will be unable to help you enroll at Millersville."

Bob was really upset. "Are you sure you can't help me?" Remember, you have always said I would be provided with enough money to pay my first years expenses."

"Yes, I expected to help, but with the business in terrible shape, due to the depression, I can't help you right now. In fact business isn't getting any better."

"Well, I guess I'll go home and explain the problem to my mother."

• • •

Arriving home at 11:30, Bessie who was doing the weekly wash, stopped and looking surprised started questioning her son.

"Why aren't you at Millersville? Did you leave early?"

"Well, Jerry refused to honor his promise, I guess I will just have to wait until I can get enough money to enroll next year."

"Wait a minute, let's discuss this before we give up. Perhaps Aunt Jessie and Uncle Jake could help you get started."

Later, talking to his aunt and uncle they told him they didn't have enough to help, but they would take out a loan for $120.

"All you have to do is pay 6% interest until you can finish payment."

"Thanks a lot! That will get me started and I am sure something will turn up."

• • •

Reaching the school the following day, he paid for tuition and books. His schedule called for 18 credits. History, Math,

English, Geography, Music and Art were scheduled for the first semester. Classes were held on Monday, Thursday and Friday with Assembly on Tuesday.

Physical Education was held on Thursday.

Since Bob was a day student, he went the twelve miles to school with friends who lived in town.

Settling into the routine schedule he discovered most of the professors to be outstanding individuals. Bob's favorite instructor was Professor George, the History teacher. He always looked forward to class, since Bob had decided he wanted to be a Historian.

Professor George told many stories about going to the Library of Congress and spending time discovering little known facts about the struggle for Independence. Quite often he had his students avidly listening to his very enthusiastic lectures.

Miss Henson, the English instructor, favored the men students for some reason. However, she expected good work from all her students.

Mr. Jensen was a math whiz. His explanations were always right on the money.

Mr. Hooper was a teacher of the old school. He expected his pupils to cover the assigned work thoroughly. Often after a student tried to beat around the bush, he would stop them.

"What does the book say?"

If anyone tried to fool him a time or two, he would call on the individual daily until they either answered him correctly or he told them to sit down and stop wasting the time of the class.

Bob studied diligently and when finals were given he memorized key portions of the book. Actually, his mark for the semester was 93. However, he always felt that the psychology course was flawed. In fact, he forgot most of what he had studied.

Mr. Johnson, the Geography instructor, hired Bob as a part time government worker, assigned to Millersville. He worked on map outlines, and marked cities, rivers and mountains. After listing all the items, Andy, using colored crayons, proceeded to finish the maps over several years.

Miss Sansone, the Art teacher, illustrated how art should be taught to elementary classes. She was very patient and understanding.

Mr. Sutler taught the Music Appreciation Class. Bob had a rough time until he figured out how he could get a good mark. Never having any back ground in any kind of classical music, he played the first few opening bars of various world famous composers. After finally memorizing the opening music he was able to fill in the name of the composer, list his birth date, explain where he lived and how he was able to perform in operas all over the music world. However, although Bob received a 92, he never really felt he deserved such a mark.

Physical Education was featured by the sports director. No one was excused, unless they had a serious health problem. Bob wasn't too keen about exercising.

Dr. Jordan was an outstanding Biology teacher. His lectures were fantastic and he had his students listening attentively in all his classes.

Unfortunately, he was at times very forgetful. Once, when he arrived at Millerville he stopped at the town post office. However, he absentmindedly left his car and walked several blocks to his classroom. Not finding his car where he usually parked it, he notified the police that his car was stolen. His car was returned to him the next morning.

All day students ate their lunch in the Old Main Building. Some students spent more time there than they did in going to classes.

One student never seemed to go to class very often. Tom would be found gambling almost everyday. His father was a director in several local companies. He supplied Tom with a new car every year.

Several day students made enough money playing cards with Tom that they paid all their expenses during four years at the school.

Most of Bob's classes were located on the fourth floor of the Old Main Building.

Underneath the classrooms was a large auditorium where all students were expected to attend Chapel during the week. Professors checked attendance and you were only excused for valid reasons.

Men's dormitories were located on four floors to the left of the chapel. Women's rooms were to the right. In the front of the auditorium were the offices of the president and other key personnel.

Science, Industrial Arts, Geography and Library were located in other buildings on the campus. In back of Old Main was a beautiful lake filled with ducks and geese. Nearby was an athletic field and an old gymnasium.

Over four years at Millersville, Bob missed almost all extra curricular programs. He was only able to attend one basketball game and two football games. Plays and concerts were all off limits. Since Bob had to help at home, he had to give his mother whatever he earned, after paying tuition.

After his freshman year was finished. Bob was hired to work at a silk mill in Lancaster during the summer. He worked from 6:00 p.m. to 6:00 a.m. and then had to get back to Marietta, afterwards. For five weeks he couldn't seem to get any rest with the constant clacking of the machines with their spindles as they moved back and forth weaving the threads into cloth. His job was to remove the cloth when it reached a prescribed length and take it to another floor to be stored.

One morning when he returned to Marietta, he looked in the Lancaster paper and found an advertisement for help placed by Armstrong Cork Company. Telling his mother he intended to get a new job, he took the trolley to Lancaster.

Arriving at the New Holland Avenue plant of Armstrong, he applied for a position and was hired and told to report on the following Monday. Returning home he reported that he had been hired. Since it was Wednesday, he only had to report to the Silk mill for two more nights.

Monday he reported to Armstrong and worked for the last 3 years while attending Millersville. In the beginning Bob was on the 3 to 11 p.m. shift. Leaving the factory, he took a trolley to Hamilton Watch Factory. Since the last trolley left Lancaster at 11 p.m. Bob had to hitchhike. First he had to get to Columbia where he had to make other connections home. During the years he worked at Armstrong, he always managed to get home by 1 a.m. At 7 a.m. he ate breakfast, and his friend Walt took him to school for his classes.

· · ·

Starting his sophomore year, Bob continued working part time for Mr. Johnson, working on the instructors many maps.

During his lunch hour he usually spent about 30 minutes playing table tennis. It was about the only time he really enjoyed himself during the week.

In October Bob was shifted to the 11 p.m. to 7 a.m. shift at Armstrong. This meant he stayed in Lancaster with former friends from Marietta until it was time for work. As a result he didn't have to rush to work and often stayed at school to prepare assignments given by the different professors.

Arriving in Lancaster, he slept for about 5 or 6 hours and then had a good meal in a nearby restaurant. He always scheduled his time to arrive at work about 10:45. Finishing his shift at 7, he caught a bus to Millersville.

· · ·

Bob looked forward to the May Day activities. One of his classmates was chosen May Queen. All the girls were decked out in beautiful dresses and danced around the May Pole. It was a great tradition that had been part of the program for years. Unfortunately it was eliminated a few years later.

• • •

May and Jay Herr had a niece at Millersville while Bob was there. Since she was in another class, he never had a chance to meet her. One morning while reading the Lancaster paper, he found her picture on the front page. While returning home from a Christian meeting in Philadelphia, she was killed instantly in a terrible wreck.

Since May and Jay Herr had helped his family during the Depression, Bob decided to go to the funeral parlor all three nights to show his respect. Naturally, he wasn't able to get any sleep. On Friday, the day of the funeral, he stayed late into the evening at school finishing up some class work that he had neglected during the week. After working at Armstrong Friday he returned home Saturday morning.

"Mom, please call me a 6:30 tonight. I have been invited for dinner at Miss Eschleman's house. You know we helped move her furniture to the second floor. It's a thank you dinner,"

"Okay, I will see that you get up in time."

At 6:30 Bessie called Bob three times. Finally going upstairs she saw he was half dressed sprawled on the bed. Covering him with a blanket, she left him to sleep, knowing he was completely bushed.

Finally, after 25 hours of sleep, Bessie at last awakened Bob.

"Why didn't you call me last night?"

"Well I called you three times and when I went up to your room, you were really sacked out."

• • •

Bob went to school during the summer so he was eligible to graduate in January.

However, he took extra credits, so he would qualify as a teacher in the secondary field, as well as the elementary grades.

• • •

Mid-term exams were scheduled for his class for the third week in January.

However, he encountered a hazing problem at Armstrong. Appearing for work at 3 p.m. he was told to check into a new department. It was called the Extrusion Department. Bob was given instructions about taking care of two large extrusion machines. It was his job to keep the hoppers on the machine filled with finely ground cork and chemicals. He was assigned to two machines.

Both machines moved back and forth, causing all 60 cylinders, one inch in diameter to solidify the cork and push it out until it reached over 3 feet at which time Bob using a sharp curved knife, cut the rods and placed them on carriers, that were later baked and sliced on machines. Eventually, they were placed inside metal bottle caps used to seal soda bottles.

Between 3 and 4 p.m., Bob placed his knife down, while replenishing the hoppers with cork. Going back for his knife, he discovered it was covered with oil and grease. Saying nothing he continued working.

While leaning over the table cutting the rods, the shift foreman came up behind Bob with an air hose and turned it on at high pressure.

Bob collapsed and was picked up and laid on some bags filled with cork. No one reported the incident. About 6 p.m. Bob finally came to. He felt excruciating pain in his abdomen. No one offered to help or call a doctor. Finally, at 11 p.m. when the shift was over, Bob staggered out of the building and caught the local trolley which took him to his physician.

After explaining what had happened, he examined Bob with a fluoroscope. He told Bob that the Lord was with him. When the air hit his body, it could have ruptured his intestines and killed him. However, the air passed through the wall, leaving 4 pockets of air in his body. It took 2 weeks for the air to disappear. Bob had lots of pain.

Bob's doctor reported the incident to Armstrong and the one responsible was fired. Bob came into work for two weeks, but didn't do anything. He kept going out to school, but spent all day in one of his friend's room on campus. Needless to say he never told his mother until he came home for the weekend.

Thinking about what happened, Bob decided that the reason no one helped him was that everyone was afraid of losing their position. During the Depression, anyone who had a job felt blessed and just let things ride. Years later Bob checked with the company just to hear what they would say about the incident. He was told it was long ago, the department was abolished, and they were not responsible for anything that happened.

• • •

Since Bob had missed his final exams for the first semester, he took each test later with the individual instructors.

At the end of May, Bob graduated with the class of 1939. It was time for his fellow graduates to start finding a teaching position.

Chapter Four

Worlds Fair

Immediately following graduation day at Millersville Bob visited the Naval base at Philadelphia. Having applied for a commission, he was given a thorough physical. Had he passed he would have taken basic training and then probably been sent to Hawaii. However his eyes were not acceptable and he was rejected.

Several weeks later he attempted to enlist in the Army. Once again he was rejected and classified 4-F, unfit for service. This rankled him for quite a spell.

. . .

During the summer of 1939, he visited the great New York World's Fair in Flushing, Long Island. In addition he visited many museums and historical places.

Returning home he informed his mother, "I'm going to get a job at the World's Fair in 1940."

• • •

During the summer of '39 he continued his employment at Armstrong. Working as a laborer in the factory, he had actually received $1,800.00 for the year.

For eight months his salary as a teacher was set at $800.00. Many of his friends figured he had gone off his rocker. At times, for the next few years, he almost agreed with their prognosis.

Five candidates had applied for the teaching position in the Rheems Public School. All had given their resumes and all had a personal interview with the board. Bob was selected for the position.

Rheems School was divided into two large rooms. On the east side Grades I through IV were taught. Grades V through VIII were assigned to Bob.

Before opening day, books and other supplies were carefully checked. Everything was in readiness for the 38 pupils when they arrived.

Rheems was a small community about 8 miles from Marietta. Quite a number of the parents were farmers. A few were employed by the local feed mill. All the parents were well acquainted. It was a close-knit group with the parents interested in furthering their children's education.

• • •

As the students entered the classroom Bob seated them according to the class in which they had been assigned. With eight rows of desks each class was given two rows, starting from the left. On the blackboard Bob wrote his name, and under it placed his inflexible rule - "Nothing for Nothing." .

After the final bell rang, everyone listened to a chapter in the Bible. It was followed by a short prayer and finished with a salute to "Old Glory."

Books were given to all students, followed by instructions telling them that all subjects were to be completed during the school day. If there were any questions, they could be asked during recess or during the lunch hour.

School day was over 6 hours, with an hour for lunch. History, Spelling, Mathematics and Geography were allotted 10 minutes for each class. Recess in the morning and afternoon was also a ten-minute period. That left about 40 minutes for Health and Music each day and 40 minutes on alternate days for Penmanship and Physical Education.

With four classes in one room it was absolutely essential that everyone cooperated and remained as quiet as possible. If anyone needed to go to the rest room, they quietly left their seats. Using the honor system and cooperation, classes were able to make substantial progress.

Eighth grade students were required to take an examination in order to enter high school in the fall.

Each month a PTA meeting was held in the evening. At that time any problems that had arisen with students were discussed. Any weakness was always mentioned and with the full support of the parents, solutions were always worked out.

• • •

Every day started at 7 a.m. with the arrival at Rheems. Whenever the coal had burned out during the night it was necessary to use paper and kindling to start the fire before the students arrived.

Twice during the school year the Assistant County Superintendent of Schools visited Rheems. At that time an opportunity arose for discussion concerning any new ideas or orders that were to be carried out. All teachers were graded on performance.

During recess and lunch games were played. Physical education was held with all classes participating.

• • •

Finishing the school term the first of May, Bob proceeded to New York for the summer. The World's Fair was due to open for the second year at the end of May.

For three weeks Bob applied for various positions at the Fair. He was unsuccessful. Finally grand opening day arrived. Bob was in the Fair Grounds when President FDR talked at the opening ceremonies. This was his second chance to see

President Roosevelt. He had listened when the president had talked to over 100,000 citizens at the Seventy Fifth anniversary of the Battle of Gettysburg. It was a noteworthy event that was held in July during a protracted heat spell.

• • •

About 5 p.m. Bob proceeded to the amusement zone. He had not been accepted for three weeks. Reaching the Pokerino building, the manager called him and explained he had been calling him several times to come to work.

"When do you want me to start?"

"Right away. I need you right now."

"Okay. I'm ready. What do you want me to do?"

"Here's an apron with lots of quarters and dollar bills. All you have to do is make change, so the customers can play the games."

Starting immediately, he was employed for the entire summer. His dream of working at the great New York World's Fair was complete.

• • •

During the next three months, he spent a good part of his time at the fairgrounds. Entering the gates at 10 a.m. he proceeded to the General Motors exhibit at once. Sitting on chairs on a moving belt he watched breathlessly as the future of transportation unfolded before his very eyes.

Future highways were shown with many new ideas. Roads were featured with circles and highway crossing over others. Everything illustrated had been in use for years, but the vision shown at the Fair was outstanding. Airports were also pictured for the future. Cars were displayed with many new ideas that are common today. An undersea world was shown that specifically portrayed the coming world. Without a doubt another great showcase was the General Electric building. First you entered a theater building with many seats. The old iceboxes, stoves, and other old-fashioned utensils were featured. Everyone was on the turntable, which moved to the next exhibit.

Every time the theater turned a new exhibit was spotlighted. After a complete turn the passengers either got off or else completed their journey again. At the Ford exhibit Fair visitors were shown the latest type of cars. In addition they were given a chance to ride in the latest models.

Kodak provided many beautifully illustrated pictures. Japan's exhibit showcased a fantastic flower and garden arrangement.

• • •

The Worlds Fair theme for 1939 was "Building The World of Tomorrow." For 1940 the theme was "For Peace and Freedom." Highlighting the fair grounds were two great units. The Trylon was a 3-sided obelisk 610 feet in height. It was taller than the Empire State Building. The round Perisphere was 18 stories high. On the inside it was twice the size of the Radio City Music Hall.

Norman Bel Geddes was responsible for the General Motors Futurama.

From the Lagoon of Nations a great fountain arose. At night it was bathed in beautiful lighting. Around 9 p.m. an eye opening fireworks extravaganza was featured nightly.

• • •

France was beaten by the Nazis who were poised to invade England. Polls taken that summer featured 50% who believed Hitler would win the war. About 70% thought that the United States was in great danger. Over three fourths wanted the Draft to be imposed on our Country.

During 1940 New York had 8 daily newspapers and 35 foreign language dailies.

• • •

In the amusement zone the Parachute ride was displayed. It provided 90 seconds of thrills. Billy Rose's Aquacade was a great highlight featuring a water show with musical accompaniment. It included various swimming formations with diving and great acrobatics. Ethel Merman was outstanding in a great musical. American Jubilee played host to thousands of visitors. Newsreels featured the World's Fair and proclaimed it as the "greatest peacetime project ever undertaken."

• • •

Robert Moses had reshaped the face of New York City. During his tenure he finished the Tri-Borough Bridge, Henry Hudson, and Marina Parkways. In addition he was responsible for over 100 smaller bridges.

However as executive director of the New York World's Fair, he put New York City and the World's Fair on the map as the greatest attraction the world had ever known. No World's Fair before or since could ever measure up to the high standards he set.

• • •

Bob spent many hours exploring many places in the city. He started by going to the Statue of Liberty in New York Harbor. Going up the first 10 stories was fairly easy. However, in order to reach the observation deck it was necessary to walk up 12 stories of circular stairways to get there. The view of the harbor and city was great.

Returning to Battery Park, the Old United States Custom building was visited. Next stop was Frances Tavern where Washington had dined quite often. On the second floor a museum featured many items about the "Father of Our Country."

Going north on Broadway, a stop was made at Trinity Cathedral, the oldest church in the city. Wall Street, the financial capital of America was checked out.

Reaching City Hall of New York another stop was made.

• • •

Across from City Hall Bob entered a Horn and Hardart Cafeteria. It was intriguing for Bob, an unsophisticated yokel to put nickels and quarters into the various cabinets and receive a beef pie, coffee, or dessert. Whenever he encountered another cafeteria in the restaurant chain, it was time for another visit.

If it was early evening, he wandered into the Bowery and Chinatown. Many times homeless people would beg for money. However, when the offer was made to take them for a meal, they often walked away. Bob never turned anyone down if they needed food, but they had to accompany him to a restaurant.

Walking up Fifth Avenue another stop was made at the Empire State Building.

Riding the elevator, visitors reached the Observation Deck. At least 40 minutes was spent looking east, west, north, and south. Using a mounted telescope brought the World's Fair into view. Other places of interest included the RCA building, Central Park, various museums, and the George Washington Bridge.

• • •

After walking in Central Park Bob found himself at the Metropolitan Museum of Art. It was a notable visit.

Exploring great art exhibits with special emphasis on the great masters was especially satisfying. Bob was particularly interested in examples of the armor equipment worn by Middle

Age combatants. Ancient artifacts, especially from Egyptian Tombs, drew his attention.

• • •

One day started with a visit to the American Museum of Natural History. As a history buff Bob first headed for the extensive dinosaur exhibit. Here were displayed fossil reptile skeletons of giant species that must have weighed between 40 and 50 tons.

On the first floor of the museum were found many giant stuffed animals that had been donated by President Teddy Roosevelt. After leaving the presidency the former Chief Executive had gone to Africa hunting Big Game. Each animal in the exhibit was placed in their former natural setting and looked almost life like.

• • •

Sometimes in the morning and early afternoon Times Square was given the once over. Several visits were made to the Paramount Theater. Frank Sinatra was the featured attraction. In order to get in moviegoers had to come early. At times the ticket line was several blocks long.

When Frank made his appearance, the bobby-sockers went bananas. Some danced in the aisles. Others yelled and a number passed out.

Nearby the Roxy Theatre put on a stage show, in addition to good movies.

At the Radio City Music Hall, patrons watched first run movies and were entertained by the world renowned Rockettes. Beautiful and talented young ladies performed intricate formations as a group, including tap dancing and coordinated high kicking.

• • •

After accepting a teaching position in his hometown, Marietta, Bob returned weekends to the World's Fair. His love affair with the World's Fair and New York City would last a lifetime. Finally in October, the last day of the Fair, Bob watched the closing ceremonies. According to the immense time clock over 500,000 fair-goers came to help close out the great Fair. This was a day that many people dreaded. Most, including Bob, felt as if a great friend had just passed away.

It was a fitting climax to a world exposition that was never duplicated.

Chapter Five

Alaska

Beginning his second year of teaching Bob was assigned the 7th Grade in Marietta. With 45 students he started the first day by discussing the goals he had set for his class. Placing his name on the board, he also wrote his "inflexible rule" underneath.

"Nothing for Nothing."

Almost all of his students' names were known. They, in turn, had often called him by his first name. No one ever used it during class work.

• • •

In addition to teaching, his duties included coaching the Junior High Basketball team. Once or twice a week he was assigned to a study hall in the High School. The school year was nine months and the salary was set at $1125.00.

Classes were allotted 45 minutes each. Specialists, at which time Bob took care of the study hall, covered physical education and music.

Once, while covering the sophomore class, Bob's sister and her friend started yapping.

"Will you please stop talking, so others can study."

Looking displeased they stopped. Later, at home, Jenny told Bessie about it.

"Were you talking and disturbing the class?"

"Well maybe we were. But he shouldn't have embarrassed us.

"Your brother was right. You're not in school to talk. Next time, behave yourself "

• • •

In late September, Bob had gone back to Armstrong, working at his former position. This helped his mother and sisters, since he made twice as much as he did teaching.

News that one of his teachers had taken another job was reported to the president of the school board.
Determined to make an example of his recently hired teacher, he contacted the County Superintendent of Schools.

JOURNEY OF FAITH_____ 63

He demanded that he fire Bob.

"Is there anything wrong with his teaching?"

"Nothing, so far."

"Since his record is satisfactory, I am unable to grant your demand."

Not satisfied with stabbing Bob in the back, he called the personal director at Armstrong.

Explaining the situation, the president of the board asked him to fire Bob.

Once again he was vehemently turned down.

Both the superintendent and personnel manager called and informed Bob of their reaction.

After seething for a few weeks, he decided to take action. Waiting until the next board meeting, Bob went to the board's office and sat in a chair outside. Several members of the board asked him what he wanted. They were told that he had something to discuss with them.

Finally he was sent for and given a seat directly facing the board's president.

Looking directly at him, he started talking.

"Gentlemen, it's come to my attention that a member of this board had demanded that I be fired because I am employed at another position. Not only was the County Superintendent of Schools contacted, but the personnel manager at

Armstrong was called."

"I'd like to make a statement. It's true that I am working at a second job. I intend to cover both positions, until my salary as a teacher in Marietta is equal to or more that I receive from Armstrong."

"Now gentlemen, does everyone understand my position? Thank you for giving me an opportunity to set the record straight."

• • •

Everything settled into a regular routine until the third week in January. Helping the students place the basket in front of the stage, somehow it fell and hit Bob on his left leg below the knee. It left a bruise about the size of a quarter on it. Checking with his local physician he tried various remedies. Nothing worked. However the bruise enlarged until it was a hard scab 2 1/2 inches by 4 1/2 inches.

Finally his doctor scheduled an appointment with a specialist in Lancaster.

Arriving about 7 he was finally ushered into the office. Pulling down an old medical book the doctor found the information he wanted.

Mixing up a concoction that looked like axle grease, he put it on the leg and bandaged it.

"Come back next week and I'll take care of it."

Arriving back at the specialist's office, the bandage was removed.

Taking a surgical knife, he lifted it off the leg.
"You have scleroderma. It's a disease in which the skin be-comes hard and rigid."

Taking a small hammer, the doctor struck the scleroderma hard. There was nothing that even showed a mark on it.

It would be 48 years later when Bob read an article in the Parade magazine about scleroderma in which an appeal was made for funds for the Scleroderma Foundation.

• • •

During the summer of 1942, Bob resigned and was ac-cepted as a trainee at Olmstead Field in Middletown. After 4 months training an opportunity for volunteers in Alaska was posted on the bulletin board. Naturally his mother and younger sister opposed the move.

At last he joined a group of 18 men with bags ready for transport by bus to Harrisburg. Arriving there, they were as-signed to a Pullman car and left for Chicago.

Since Bob had never been anywhere in the mid-west, he was anxiously watching as the train passed the famous Horse-shoe Curve of the Pennsylvania Railroad. Next morning, after eating breakfast, the train pulled into the Chicago Station.
Later they embarked on the Great Northern Railroad that was to take them all the way to Seattle. Their group was given an entire car with Pullman service the entire way.

They were treated royally, since travel was restricted. The porter provided anything they wanted. As the group passed small towns and cities, they were given all sorts of information about the country.

About every 100 miles or so, the train was stopped and a new engine was hooked up. The journey then continued.

It was very interesting to watch as the train passed through the Northern Plains. Stops were usually made to take on water.

Some of the volunteers spent most of their time playing poker. Others read books and magazines.

Most of the way there was only one track. So the train would pull into a siding until a train going east passed. Continuing on they reached Glacier National Park. It was snowing heavily and the double engines really had to work hard to take the cars up and around the mountains.

After 3 days they arrived in Seattle and settled into their hotel rooms. It was discovered the boat taking them to Anchorage would not leave for a week.

Ten from the group seemed to prefer wasting time in beer joints. Others were looking for girls. One individual, who boasted about his way with women, and what he did, evidently needed a long rest on the boat trip.

At last they embarked on their boat and started on their journey up the coast.

Traveling the inside passage, they passed many islands and

the boat ride was smooth. The islands protected the boat from violent ocean waves.

Meals were excellent, with plenty to eat. A brief stop was made at Ketchikan; a small village built on hills surrounding the shore. Another brief stop was made at Juneau, the capital of Alaska. Next the boat headed out to the Pacific Ocean.

Big waves violently rocked the boat. Most of the group, including Bob were seasick.

After a time the boat entered Cook Inlet, where the shoreline helped cut down the high waves.

At last they cruised into the port at Anchorage. About 10 p.m. all left the boat with equipment and were taken to a G.I. dining hall where they were supplied with food.

• • •

Afterward. they were taken to Army tents, which were heated with coal stoves.
Everyone was informed that someone had to keep the fire burning. Unfortunately several didn't get up and tend it.

Everyone awakened to find the tent below zero. Needless to say everyone dressed in record time.

After eating all moved into one of the large hangers where they stayed for a day.

Finally they were sent to Anderson's Camp. Most everyone called it Anderson's Rat Hole.

In the shower icicles hung from the ceiling. Bob appropriated an old tub and washed in his cubbyhole room.

Many construction workers on the Alcan Highway were quartered at Anderson's Camp. It was their first encounter with a rough crew.

At mealtime, especially breakfast, everyone looked out for themselves. Big platters of pancakes were placed on each table. If someone was slow, by the time he caught on, the plate would be empty. This was true of all meals.

• • •

Disgusted with the accommodations at Anderson's, everyone packed their bags and headed for the hangar. After a delay, they were given the use of the second floor in a barrack. Quite a friction developed between the "G.I's" and the "Feather Merchants" on the second floor.

Most of the men understood the resentment. Airmen, working with them were making $50.00 a month, and civilians were receiving at least $5,000.00 a year.

• • •

Although all their training in the states was concerned with aircraft parts, several of them found themselves taking inventory at the base.

Fifteen scattered warehouses off the base at Anchorage had

to be checked. There was usually no record of what had been put there. An old Master Sergeant (35 years service) had unloaded ships at Cook Inlet and taking Army trucks filled the warehouses.

At times it was necessary to consult blueprints to find out what part was stored away. Outside the buildings they found piles of 55-gallon drums of gasoline. They had been dumped in the woods. Only the Sergeant knew where they were placed.

Once they discovered a pile of Aircraft heaters about 40 feet high. Heaters on the bottom were useless as they were stuck in the mud.

Another time they found two perfectly good pontoons. It took two months to figure out they were for a Canadian Seaplane.

A $25,000.00 aircraft engine had been dumped outside. It was a complete loss.

At another time Bob was filling out an order for a nut and bolt for a fighter plane in the Aleutians. Sixteen copies were made of the order. Two copies would have been enough. No one ever found out where the other copies showed up.

• • •

Usually several members from Olmstead went to a small Methodist church in Anchorage. The employees who had been assigned the second floor of the Army barracks will long remember Christmas Eve. On the bulletin board was a notice telling them to evacuate their rooms, since G.I.'s were moving in.

After much discussion, every person decided to visit Anchorage and not to move out until the day after Christmas. Packing their belongings, they moved back to the hangar.

Bob and three men from the group rented a cabin, about a mile from the airfield.

What a tragic mistake. Two of them were habitual saucers.

A Yukon stove was in the middle of the kitchen. Filling it with wood lasted all night. It was up to Bob and Jake, the odd men, to keep the fire going and see that a supply of wood was always on hand.

Since the privy was 100 feet from the house, the seats were always frozen. No one dared to sit down, because you would be stuck on the seat. So using the same technique as they did during the depression days, they squatted.

● ● ●

After one month, Jake and Bob high-tailed out of their cabin and rented a smaller cabin, a little closer to the base. It was equipped with a stove hooked up to a tank outside. Using oil from the planes, they managed to keep fairly warm.

Things went along swimmingly for a few months. All meals were eaten in the Officer's Mess. Many times Jake, who was a Mennonite, often discussed different viewpoints with Bob, a Presbyterian. Quite often the talks became somewhat heated.

Once while walking to the cabin, Bob discovered a big bear blocking the path.

Although it was snowing, he quickly circled around some trees. Probably the bear was saturated with food from the base, but it seemed sensible to avoid an encounter.

• • •

For a period of two weeks there was a shortage of oil for the base. Naturally, they kept flying the planes out until new shipments arrived. However, that left Jake and Bob in a pickle.

Using a little ingenuity, they collected two sleeping bags from the base's hangar. Since they were the old-fashioned button types they opened both and laid one on the bed. Taking the second bag they hooked it on top of the bottom bag, leaving just enough room to keep their heads out. Next they removed their clothing, placed it under themselves and slept on it. When morning arrived both dressed in the sleeping bags.

• • •

Several times Bob had taken physicals to see if he could pass the eye exam. In 1939 his eyes resulted in 20/800. Now according to the physician he had improved to 20/200. Of course the fact he had memorized the chart helped.

After ruminating for several days he decided he was going home and would try one more time to get in the service.

Resigning from his civil service position, he waited for transportation to the states. Finally, he was assigned a seat alongside lots of baggage. As the two-engine Curtiss took off the rains came down in torrents.

It didn't last very long. With the sunshine very bright, traveling at 10,000 feet, everyone was enjoying the beautiful landscape as they flew over thousands of islands. It reminded the passengers that it looked like a great postcard with forest trees interspersed with crystal clear water with patches of cumulus clouds really making it fantastic.

• • •

Arriving at Seattle, all passengers were bumped off to make room for several aircraft engines. The next day at 10 a.m., a flight became available. A stop was made at Spokane. Once again they had to make room for special equipment.

About 3 in the afternoon, a loud speaker called for volunteers for a B-17. Several, including Bob, volunteered. In 15 minutes the bomber was high above Spokane. Looking down at the city and the beautiful fields, they really appreciated their opportunity.

All of a sudden, some of the hitchhikers noticed that a red light, above the pilot went off and on, according to the pilot's movement. At the same time, they all noticed a black cloth had been placed over the pilot's cockpit. A sergeant, who was a member of the crew, explained they were testing radar, which allowed pilots to fly even in terrible weather conditions. At first they were bothered, but eventually started to really enjoy the trip. After 2 1/2 hours of all kinds of experimental maneuvers the pilot brought the plane down. Removing the black cloth from the cockpit the pilot landed right in the middle of the runway. Radar became a wonderful tool to help in all types of flying and precision bombing.

• • •

At eight the next morning, they connected with a flight. This time the destination was an Air Force Base at Ogden, Utah. Once again they were bumped off. Bob decide he had enough hitchhiking.

Taking a bus to Salt Lake City, he was able to get a ticket to Chicago in 20 minutes. This time they were on a Union Pacific train. A ten-hour stop was made in Kansas and a few hours layover in Chicago.

At last he was headed east and finally reached the Lancaster station the next day. Taking a trolley to Colombia, he finally reached Marietta about 10 a.m. Reaching his mother's apartment he rang the bell. When she saw her son, she hugged and kissed him.

"What are you doing here? I thought you were in Alaska. What happened?"

"Take it easy, I'll explain if you give me a chance."

As he explained he had come back to enlist in the Air Force his mother's face darkened.

"Why aren't you satisfied? You're needed as a teacher. You should be thankful you're not in the service."

"Mother it doesn't matter what you say, my mind is made up."

"How soon will you go for induction?"

"Two or three weeks at the most."

"It's time you settled down."

"No more talk. I'm going to see as many of my friends as possible, especially Eloise and her family and Jenny.

•   •   •

In three weeks, Bob left for Harrisburg. This time he vowed he would be successful.

Chapter Six

Air Force

Since he had failed four times, Bob realized it was his last chance to get rid of his 4-F status. Arriving at Harrisburg, about 50 men were taken to an examination room and were checked out physically. Most of them were approved by the attending physician. It was finally Bob's turn to have an eye examination.

Taking Bob's glasses, the doctor suggested that Bob should walk toward the eye chart. Realizing the doctor understood what he was trying to do, he stopped at the half-way distance and called out the first letter.

"Hell, if you're so anxious to get in the service, I'll pass you." The induction papers were signed. Later they took the oath of allegiance. In the afternoon all who passed were bussed to the New Cumberland Staging Area. From there the new inductees would be sent to boot camp for assignment.

The "feather merchant" that had rankled him in Alaska

was buried at long last.

Uniforms and other service equipment were issued to the new recruits. They all realized that they were now GIs.

Lying in his bunk, Bob had a squeamish feeling in his stomach as he realized that he was on his own and subject to Army rules and regulations.

During the second day he was assigned to K-P duty. Although a necessary part of their training, it never went over big with most servicemen.

Orders were cut for 200 recruits to report at Gulfport Air Base for 13 weeks of very intensive training. All were carried on a train of the Southern Railroad. When they arrived, they discovered that it was going to be as hot as blazes during their summer training.

Starting with reveille in the morning all were on the move until chow time. Drill instructors constantly pushed until most of the men were almost completely exhausted and then pulled on something extra.

Saturday mornings were extra special. The entire squad was taken on what was billed as a 10 mile long hike. It involved half-running and half walking. As a bonus, gas was thrown alongside the marchers. Everyone had been taught how to put on the gas masks. If anyone passed out, they were placed in an ambulance and taken to the base hospital. Of course they missed a chance to visit New Orleans.

At 3 p.m. all were marched to the parade grounds and stood at attention in the broiling sun for what seemed an eternity, but actually was about 15 minutes. Quite a few would pass out.

No one helped them. Later they were carted off to the base hospital where they stayed until Monday morning.

Leaving the base at 4:30 p.m. they were bussed to the Southern Railway station. Tickets were purchased (half-fare) and the train departed for New Orleans at 5:30.

Lakes, swamps, and bays were crossed. No one seemed to mind. Everyone was looking forward to a night in the great city on the Mississippi River.

Arriving after 8 o'clock, most immediately headed for Charity Hospital, a newly constructed facility. Since it was only opened, many rooms were empty. GIs were allowed to rent a room for 50 cents. The hospital featured all the comforts of home, including air conditioning, something most of the servicemen had never encountered at home.

After checking in at Charity, GIs went out on the town. Some made a night of it, but others visited the French Quarter. Bob was intrigued with the outstanding wrought iron work on the balconies.

On Sunday some went to church, usually going to different churches each week.

Pumping stations were in operation day and night. It was absolutely essential that the pumps were continuously in action, because the city was actually two feet below the Mississippi River.

In the cemeteries bodies were buried four or five on top of each other. Those on the bottom were completely under water.

Several old churches and museums were open for weekends for tourists and military personnel. Steamboats were on a daily schedule going up the Mississippi.

One Sunday Bob visited Lake Ponchartrain. It covers 630 square miles. It's linked with the great river via canal and is connected with the Gulf of Mexico with Lake Borgne.

During the summer several hundred soldiers who had eaten tainted food in the mess hall, came down with ptomaine poisoning. They spent the best part of the night in the latrines bringing up the poisonous food they had eaten. Most everyone was deathly sick. Most of the mess officers were held responsible and lost their rating as officers. Inspection increased with high level supervision.

At the end of basic training, Bob along with 15 others, was assigned to Camp Lee, Virginia. Although Camp Lee was a Quarter Master training center, members of the Air Force were instructed on how to supply aircraft parts.

While at Camp Lee, many interesting individuals were met. One soldier really made quite an impression. George owned 4 restaurants in the Minneapolis-St. Paul area. Every week, while, at Camp Lee, he had several boxes, with all kinds of food and goodies sent for the entire barracks. However, he was very bitter. At 44 he had been dumped in the service. Before we left Camp Lee he provided everyone with a complete turkey dinner with all the trimmings.

One year later we heard that he was digging ditches in the

islands. He never cooperated with the Air Force. Finally we received word that he had been killed. What a waste of a fine gentleman and a successful businessman.

Every weekend Bob received a pass to Richmond. There were many outstanding historical places to visit. Along the main thoroughfare were statues of great Southern generals, including Robert E. Lee, and Stonewall Jackson.

Virginia's state capitol building was well worth a visit. There were also museums. St John's church was where Patrick Henry spoke a few eloquent words about the colonies.

"Give me liberty or give me death."

A man who was willing to give his life for his belief in the American dream.

Large cemeteries where both the Blue and Gray were buried, along with two United States Presidents, James Monroe and Zachary Taylor.

After New Years 1944, Bob was transferred to the 406th Fighter Group. He was assigned to the 513th Fighter Squadron at the Congaree Air Base in South Carolina. Since the squadron already had a full complement of non-commissioned officers, he would remain as a Pfc. for over a year, as an aircraft supply clerk.

Lt. Jason was the Supply Officer, who gave his approval on all requisitions. Sgt. Joe was a former hill-billy from Texas, who was obsessed with his own importance. Next in the supply group was Sgt. Henson who became Bob's best friend. Always ready with a smile, he kept things cool. Corporal Wood, who had a shock of bright red hair, rounded out the squadron supply personnel.

After a few weeks, the entire group moved to Myrtle Beach. Engineers had laid out a runway of light steel before anyone arrived.

The 406lh Fighter Group had been given 75 P-47s, 25 each to the 512th, 513th and 514th Fighter Squadrons. Pilots took off from the runway, headed for targets, made simulated attacks, and returned to base. This was advanced training which gave pilots much needed experience that could be applied when the outfit reached the European Theatre of Operations.

One night Sgt. Joe came into the supply tent, soused to the gills. Talking a blue streak, he suddenly decided to eliminate some of the beer in his bloated bladder. He moved towards Bob, who picked up a brick, to stop Joe before he could spray the tent.

"Don't you dare urinate in the tent. If you do, you're going to have a slight dent in your head."

Joe went outside, but he held a grudge against Bob for over two years.

Returning to Congaree, the Group prepared to move. When orders were received, the group was sent to a staging area. Prior to their arrival, all personnel had receive shots for smallpox, typhoid and tetanus. Actually, all members of the group were merely marking time.

Before embarking on a former English cruise ship, every GI received a Red Cross packet, along with a donut and coffee. Leaving the pier, the ship moved slowly into the Hudson River. Passing the majestic Statue of Liberty, almost everyone remained silent. No doubt most of them were wondering if they would ever see America again. Entering into Atlantic Ocean, the silence gave way to lots of noises as things returned to normal. For the next two weeks the cruise ship served as home. Over 5,000 were packed in like sardines. Over 50 boats, with Navy destroyers, provided cover, along with submarines. Following a zigzag pattern they headed south, following the East Coast of Africa and moving north, passed the French Coast, and arrived in England.

Food served on the boat, to put it mildly, was practically worthless. Bob couldn't stomach lamb, and that's what was served many times during the voyage. When the ocean acted up, you had to hold your tray or your food was deposited on the floor.

Luckily for some of the soldiers, the boat had a well stocked commissary. Some, including Bob, bought a case of 24 cans of sliced pineapples. Whenever lamb was served, they opened a can. Actually, the only decent meal that they enjoyed was when hot dogs highlighted the menu.

While on board several enterprising individuals ran games of chance. Games continued day and night. It seemed like the only person who made out like a bandit, was the person running the game. Every day, several thousand dollars was locked in the ship's safe. The take was over $20,000, not bad for a weeks worth of work.

After several sub scares the convoy reached Southampton. Leaving the boat Red Cross girls handed out coffee and donuts.

A long troop train carried the 406th Fighter Group to Ashford in Kent. Engineers had already constructed a metal runway and the pilots started to fly missions over France soon after. Everyone was anticipating the coming invasion of the continent.

Hitler started launching his rockets aimed at London. The first night rumors swept the camp that the Germans had invaded England. All the GIs soon became used to the constant buzz of the rockets.

Rockets had a gyroscope in the back, which guided them to their target. Once a rocket malfunctioned and landed in a near by field. If it had hit the 406th, many lives would have been snuffed out. At times spitfires that were already airborne, hit the gyroscope causing the rocket to fall and explode.

Bob discovered that the British rarely had seen oranges. After he saved six, instead of eating them, he swapped them for a bicycle. It was taken along to France and provided him an opportunity to visit many places of interest.

While in England, some soldiers visited London. Trains regularly stopped at Ashford. Many visited the Tower of London, the Wax Museum, Westminster Abbey and St. John's Church. Admiral Nelson's monument and Buckingham Palace were places Bob had read about and was intensely interested in seeing.

Wherever soldiers congregated, ladies of the night were ready, willing and able to provide their services. Piccadilly Circus was well known in England.

One of Bob's friends from Marietta was a gunner on a B-17 bomber that exploded in England. Bob visited a family where Jim had often spent time during a break in the bombing of Germany. All they could tell him was that the B-17 had barely taken off, when it crashed and exploded, killing all those on board.

During May of 1943, fighter pilots of the 406th Group made many sorties against fortifications guarding the French coast. It was obvious that an invasion was imminent. The only question was when it would begin and what part of the coast would be invaded first.

Using 3 big Army trucks, all spare parts for the P-47s were loaded. Bob, along with the trucks, was assigned to a supply outfit that had a 200-unit company of black soldiers. Outside of a white officer, he was the only other white person in the company.

All other members of the 406th group, except the pilots, were sent ahead to wait embarkation. Bob's orders specified that he was responsible for seeing the supplies were delivered promptly.

Reaching the beach was the easy part. A lone German bomber dropped a few bombs and Bob very foolishly hid under one of the trucks. He never repeated that boo-boo. No one on the beach would share any information. For the next few weeks, Bob, with the 3 truck drivers, covered a good part of

France, near the Saint Lo area. Going through Saint Lo, he was amazed at the vast destruction in the area. The area was devastated. Allied bombers had hit their own troops, resulting in over 3,000 casualties, including Lt. General McNair. As a result Air Force officers were assigned to the Army, to pinpoint where enemy troops were encamped. Relaying the information to the Air Force resulted in pilots taking appropriate action.

At the end of the third week, they found an Air Force Officer who told Bob the 406th Group was at an airfield 2 miles away. Since it was almost 5 p.m., the truck drivers wanted to return to their base on the coast. Bob insisted that they go on, since he was certain they would need some of the vital parts for the planes.

Arriving at the airfield at Tour en Bessen, France, all trucks were unloaded in 15 minutes and the drivers returned to their company.

Next stop for the group was at Crettville, France. Some of the pilots were housed in a chateau.

Whenever the group moved, engineers had laid down a metal runway for the pilots. Arriving at Loupeland, France, the group found the French people very appreciative of their effort to knock off the little dictator.

Pilots returning after bombing and strafing found the enthusiastic French clapping and often when they returned, one or two pilots were missing. Some had been killed. Others were missing in action, later found to be prisoners of war.

Almost all of the 406th Group were sent to Mourmeland le Grande, near Rheims.

However, Bob was left behind as a member of a clean-up crew. On the second day a large Army truck arrived with a load of hams. For the rest of the 10 days the crew had ham for breakfast, lunch, and dinner. Some of the hams were swapped for eggs and chicken. Most of the local people had very little meat. Needless to say they had a ball enjoying the food. When they reached Mourmeland Ie Grande, they turned the hams over to the cooks. As far as the crew knew, no one noticed that some of the hams had flown the coup. While stationed at the former German Air Base, Bob noticed an article in the Stars and Stripes concerning the black market in cigarettes and gasoline.

For a six-week period no cigarettes reached the front lines. Several officers and enlisted men had stolen them and made a small fortune. Caught and court-martialed, some of the men were sent to the front as privates or else they could spend many years in a military prison.

Gasoline was sent to leading tank divisions by the Red Ball Express drivers. Often they sold some of the gas and arrived at their destinations with a partly filled tank. When caught they were severely punished, usually with a long prison term.

Bob couldn't understand how they could betray their country in such a brazen manner.

Everyone was housed in former Luftwaffe barracks. Pilots used the runway built by the Germans. While there the 406th was providing air cover for old "Blood and Guts," General George Patton's Third Army. Many sorties were made over

Bastogne. One of two Presidential Citations was given for the action of the great pilots in the bombing of the Bastogne area.

On New Years Eve, a few members of the group got a little tipsy and started firing their carbines. Bob promptly crawled under his bunk and covered himself with a blanket. He decided he wasn't going to be a casualty if he could help it.

Several times, while stationed at Mourmeland, Bob visited Rheim's Cathedral. It is a fine example of Gothic architecture. Many fine artisans worked for hundreds of years to finally complete a masterpiece that will stand tall for centuries.

Leaving the Luftwaffe barracks, the group moved to Metz. Having just made themselves ship-shape, orders came to move immediately. Some fine mechanical tools had just been received. Bob was ordered to dig a large hole and drop them all in it. What a waste! All the tools had been wrapped in oil for preservation. Someone in future years was certainly going to be surprised when they stumbled on them.

Passing through Luxembourg, a small independent country of about 1000 square miles, with a population of about 400,000, they arrived at Asche in Belgium, where another airfield was set up.

Using empty rocket boxes for flooring, tents were set up. Used oil from the P-47s was used in small heaters to keep the tents warm and cozy.

Although Bob was not particularly in favor of gambling, he played anyhow.
Actually, he never lost any money, because he was a careful

player.

Several times, while at Asche, Bob managed to get a pass to Brussels. While there, he visited some historic places.

Some in the administrative staff managed to get a 3-day pass to visit Paris.

Handorf, Germany, was where Bob found out he should never take a dare. Sgt. Henson dared anyone to get a moonie. Thinking his friend must be a little teched in the head, he agreed, never thinking his buddy would have all his hair cut off. The next day Sgt. Henson showed up with his head as bare as a billiard ball. Bob tried to weasel out of his agreement but he was held down and promptly sheared.

While foraging in a big barn, several members of the group dug up many cases of old champagne that had evidently been buried for a few years.

Although Bob and Sgt. Henson had never touched any liquor, they decided to celebrate whenever V-E Day arrived. Appropriating 4 bottles of champagne, they started to drink. Bob finished off one bottle and started another.

"That champagne is all right. It's like the best soda I ever tasted." However, in an hour, he rushed outside and all the champagne came up.

Sgt. Henson was sick for the entire day and never left his room. That was the last time either one drank any more liquor.

After V-E Day the entire 406th Group was transferred to

Nordholz, Germany to another former Luftwaffe base. Germans were hired to clean rooms, work in the kitchen and for various positions on the base. It was discovered that many of them were stealing whatever they could lay their hands on. Women were found concealing food in their bras and pants. Most of them were unable to buy anything because everything went into the war effort. Men were caught stealing cigarettes, candy, and tools.

With the war in Europe now over, the 406th was assigned for occupation of Germany. However, since the 406th Group had been overseas for almost 2 years, under the point system, many were eligible to start home in September.

Bob, who had never trusted the Nazis, trusted the Russians no more than the Germans. He decided to sign up for an additional 18 months to be spent in Germany watching the Russians.

Since almost all the non-commissioned men were being rotated home, Bob was made a Sgt. in September and appointed Tech/Sgt. in October with a promise of M/Sgt. in January.

In early September Bob was fortunate enough to join others from the Air Force to be the first group to be taken on a bus tour of Denmark. Starting from Bremen and driving through Lubeck they reached Sonderberg, located on the coast. Local officials greeted everyone and a wonderful dinner was provided in the hotel.

On the following day, the buses reached Odense where Danish citizens warmly welcomed everyone. The third day was spent in Arhus, a very large commercial and industrial city. It is Denmark's second largest city and one of the oldest. While there, Bob was invited to one of the homes to spend the night, but had to reluctantly refuse. He was afraid he might miss the bus, which was headed for Copenhagen in the morning.

Arriving at the dock, the entire Air force contingent boarded a very large ferry, which would carry them to the island where the capital was located. During the trip, everyone was given a fantastic meal, which featured a great roast with gobs of outstanding gravies. Bob was particularly impressed with some of the best tiny potatoes he had ever eaten.

Leaving the ferry and boarding the buses, a short stop was made at Denmark's fine cathedral, which had been built many centuries ago. At last they reached the city's best hotel. For the next three days and nights they could enjoy the city.

Most of the group ate at Copenhagen's outstanding restaurant, featuring a smorgasbord menu. Tables over 50' in length were loaded down with every kind of food imaginable, topped off with delicious desserts of all kinds-a real honest-to-goodness feast.

During the second day, after visiting a museum and watching the activity at the docks, Bob went to a dance where he met several friendly, young Danish girls. Invited to one home, he met the family and slept on a mattress laid on the floor.

A first class amusement park in the city, The Tivoli, was visited on the last day in Copenhagen. Striking up an acquaintance with a young hotel waitress, he proceeded to take all the moving rides and have a great time. Bob found out that the family didn't have much left after the Germans moved out.

Giving her some fruit, candy, and cigarettes, he told her if he ever came back on a furlough, he would try and bring her whatever the family might use.

Returning to Nordholz was non-eventful. Bob looked forward to visiting Copenhagen at another time.

Bob had been concerned with the Russians since they had hooked up with Nazis.

He felt it was important to stay on so he had re-enlisted for an additional 18 months. It was especially important for the United States to watch Stalin who had butchered millions of Russians while he was consolidating his control of the country.

Every week the GIs were given a carton of cigarettes. Since he never smoked Bob saved 10 cartons. He decided he would exchange them for a world-famous Leica Camera. He was offered a trip to Dresden with a Master Sergeant, a friend of Bobs.

After arranging a pass to Dresden, which was controlled by the British Army, they reached the city. In no time at all Bob had his Leica.

In the mean time his friend had sold 40 cartons of cigarettes for $200.00 a carton.

He had $4,000.00 in British Pound notes. Since the British Army was only allowed 10 pounds to be sent home, Bob's friend gave them $4,000.00 in British money for $8,000.00 in Occupation money. His total take for the day was $12,000.00. Not bad for a half-days work.

Black-market action of all kinds surfaced a few months after VE day. During one month American soldiers in Berlin, while receiving $3,000,000.00 sent $4,000,000.00 to the states. The following month a new order was listed by the Army Treasury Department severely curtailing any money sent home by the troops.

In November Bob received another 7-day pass to return to Denmark. Filling 2 suitcases with fruit, canned goods, and other items, he delivered all to Alicia's parents as soon as he arrived.

While in the city, Alicia showed him many places of interest. In addition she introduced him to her friends and relatives. Frankly, he enjoyed himself the entire time. Nothing serious emerged, since she was only 18 while he was almost 28.

Something had changed the attitude of some of the Danish people since his first visit. Young soldiers, many who had just entered the service, really acted obnoxious. Many were drunk almost all of the time; others were discourteous; used foul language; and generally made a bad impression on the Danish people. It made Bob feel very sorry to see what was happening.

Returning to Nordholz, he received a letter from his sister Eloise, telling him that Bessie was in bad shape, and that maybe he should try and return.

Immediately he requested a transfer to the States, after explaining the situation to his executive officer. Sent to a staging area in early January he waited for transportation. Finally, he was on his way. Two weeks later he reached the States and was sent to Fort Dix for processing.

Chapter Seven

Marriage

Bob spent the first week home on furlough, busily visiting his mother, sisters, and brother. In addition, numerous nieces, nephews and old friends were visited.

On Monday, he met an old friend who asked him if he was interested in going into partnership starting a combined restaurant and dance floor for the young people in town. Bob immediately jumped at the chance and okayed the project.

Bill, Bob's friend, drew up papers which sealed the business deal. However, Bill informed him that since he wasn't a veteran, he was unable to procure building supplies. So Bob visited various government agencies, but was also refused.

While visiting New York, where he met another set back, he decided to visit Yankee Stadium. What a fortunate turn of events. Bob witnessed a superlative game In which Bob Feller pitched a no hitter. It was his first and only game involving the Yankees that he ever attended.

Finally Bill and Bob decided to buy an old three-story hotel located on Front Street. They started with the roof, saving everything. Thousands of bricks were cleaned and many old support beams saved for the construction of the restaurant.

• • •

All the work was completed, when the Air force issued orders for Bob to report to Fort George Meade for reassignment. So Bill started construction of the restaurant without Bob's help. Arriving at Fort Meade, an evaluation was made sending him to Andrews Air Force Base in Washington D. C. He, along with other Air Force personnel, twiddled their thumbs while awaiting orders. However, Bob had a wonderful three weeks spending every day seeing everything he had always wanted to visit again. His three day tour with his class of 1935 had merely whetted his appetite for historic Washington.

First stop was Mount Vernon. It was rapidly followed by visits to National Archives; Lincoln Memorial; Washington Monument, Library of Congress; Senate; House of Representatives; Treasury Department; Botanical Gardens; Smithsonian; Art Museums; Red Cross; and other places of historic interest.

• • •

On June 5, 1946 Bob was assigned to an Air Force Reserve Unit that was stationed at Newark, N.J. With a complement of officers and enlisted men, there were about 180 individuals assigned to the unit.

While a part of the Air Reserve, Bob along with others, was sent to the YMCA for meals and individual rooms. Most of the assigned pilots lived at home.

It was Bob's job to keep pilots informed of their projected flying hours, so that they retained flying status for each month. Colonel Johnson, from Staten Island, was the head honcho of the unit. Bob found him very easy to work with at all times.

Since Bob lived at the YMCA, he ate all meals in their cafeteria. Often he noticed G.I.'s making a date with Maisie, who was the cashier and dietician. After sizing up the situation, he decided to approach her indirectly. Talking to a co-worker, he asked her to find out if Maisie was willing to visit New York on a first date. The response was immediate and Maisie and Bob got to know each other very quickly.

• • •

Leaving Newark in October 1946, the couple compared experiences. Both of them loved New York. Bob, remembering his adventures while attending New York's World Fair of 1939-1940. Maisie earned her degree as a dietician in the city.

Since each was intrigued with the Horn & Hardart restaurant chain, they always visited the shops while in the city.

After eating in the H & H near New York City Hall, Bob bought tickets on a double-decker bus and they traveled up Fifth Avenue and eventually reached Fort Tryon Park.

Walking through the park, they stopped at one of the park benches and watched the activities in the Palisade Park in New Jersey.

Since it was now 9:30, Maisie became a little alarmed. Later she explained that she held on to her pocketbook because it was to be used to clobber her date if he stepped out of line.

Returning to Newark about 11:00 p.m., they agreed to return to New York the next night. That led to another date on the third night. Going back to the park again they sat and talked for an hour until both were very quiet.

Jumping up, Bob who had a carefully prepared speech, knelt in front of Maisie. "Maisie, I know I'm rushing things a little, but my mind is made up. Will you marry me?"

"Yes, I was hoping you would make up your mind. I've been watching you for some time."

"Well to tell the truth, I've watched how you deal with other G.I.s and I felt maybe I'd have a chance with you."

Following a few (??) kisses the love birds returned to earth and reached Maisie's home by 11:30.

• • •

In the meantime, Bill and Bob's plan for a restaurant became a reality. An agreement was reached that would guarantee that Bill would receive $125.00 a week to operate the restaurant from Monday thru Friday.

Bob returned late Friday and took over on Saturday and Sunday. He was a trifle concerned with his relationship with Bill, because of mistakes he had made during the construction of their building.

First, he had tried to hide a few expenses by paying without telling Bob. Secondly, he had poured too much concrete and wasn't able to firm it up. (Save a few cents, he told Bob) For several weeks Bob spent most of his weekends chiseling off concrete that had never been handled properly. Disgusted, at last, Bob told his partner to have linoleum placed on the floor.

One day Bill told Bob that they could make more money by keeping out $20 or $30 dollars of each day's receipts. Bob, who had suspected that Bill had been holding out on daily receipts, removed his apron.

"That's enough for me. I'm walking out. You take over. I've realized you only used me to get the building. Now you can get an oil company to back you and run a service station you always wanted. Call me when you're ready."

• • •

After deciding to take the plunge, Maisie and Bob approached their families.

Maisie's sisters and friends were ecstatic. Bob's sister and brother approved, but Bessie, Bobs' mother threw a monkey wrench into the idea of marriage.

"Have you lost your mind? You haven't been back more than a few months and now you want to get married. It's too soon. Why don't you wait awhile?"

After several sessions with Bessie, Maisie and Bob decided to wait six months.

In the mean time, Bob, who commuted home each weekend, received a cold reception whenever he tried to discuss the marriage.

Bob never brought Maisie for a visit because of Bessie's objections. They discussed options. Maisie asked Bob if he felt they should forget the marriage. However, he adamantly told her that Bessie would have to accept his decision.

"Mother will be the one who loses out. Either she accepts you or I'll not talk to her after we're married. The Good Book says that you should always support your wife and start a new life with her. That's what I intend to do."

• • •

One day before Easter in 1947, Maisie and Bob were married. Bessie attended, but didn't bend. In fact she completely ignored Maisie.

"Mother, this will be my last visit without Maisie. If you don't recognize she is my wife I don't intend to see you."

Bessie continued to castigate Maisie. Bob, who stayed the first year of marriage with Maisie's sister, told her not to tell Bessie where he was in case she called and wanted information.

Bob couldn't believe what his mother was doing. Time passed. It would be 4 years before Bessie made the call and invited Maisie to her home.

During the four years Bob never returned home. It was the worst years of his life.

Knowing if he contacted his relatives or friends Bessie would continue to speak against his wife. So Bob made a complete break.

• • •

It was November of 1951 when Bessie called and suggested that Bob and Maisie come to Marietta and talk. It was a night with a blanket of fog over the East Coast. Leaving Newark at 9:00 p.m., they reached Marietta at 1:00 a.m. Bessie apologized. However, Bob's wife and mother merely tolerated each other.

Several times Bessie was invited to stay for a few weeks during summer.

However, there was always an undercurrent. Maisie's sister naturally never had any love for Bessie and so she was very short with any remarks that she made.

Bill called Bob to come and settle the partnership agreement. Bob paid off everyone he owed and in addition gave Bessie and Maisie's sister each $1,000. That left him with enough to buy a car and take a honeymoon trip later.

• • •

Enrolling at Seton Hall, Bob received an M.A, in history. While going to school he worked at Kresge's Department Store as a mail clerk.

Since Bob and Maisie had only a week-end in Washington, D.C. after marriage, they decided to take a 5 week trip on the Greyhound to Los Angeles and return. Their tickets for the round trip specified that at any stop they could get off, stay over night and get another bus the following day. Leaving Newark with lots of luggage, they started their trip. Reaching Washington, D.C. they checked into an apartment on the American University campus, leaving everything not needed for traveling.

Bob was due to return to the University at the end of August to begin studying for his degree in History with special emphasis on American History.

• • •

First stop after leaving the university was Atlanta, Georgia. For one day they checked places of historic interest. At night they traveled to the next city New Orleans.

After showering in the station, they decided to visit the French Quarter. They were much impressed with iron railings on the many old buildings, and several old churches.

Since the heat was very strong, they decided to move on to the next stop in Texas. High light of the trip was a visit to the Alamo. Bob was always a history buff, and visited many historic points.

However, Maisie was often stricken with recurring head-aches. It started when they hit Texas and continued off and on throughout the rest of the trip. Maisie insisted on continuing but it wasn't too pleasant for her.

Stops were made during the days in Arizona and New Mexico, without much visiting of important places.

Finally reaching California, they visited Los Angeles. They were hit with smog, and decided to visit San Diego. The trip down the coast was pleasant. While in San Diego, they visited Sea World and others points. Taking a local bus they went into Mexico and visited Tijuana.

It seemed to be a wide-open town. If you had the money, you could buy anything. Drugs were sold openly on the street. Many sleazy joints were jumping night and day.

While walking around, Bob was often accosted by little urchins asking for money.

Maisie found out that you should never pay the quoted price. Often it saved her several dollars.

• • •

William Randolph Hearst's castle was the next stop on their trip. Visiting the mansion and listening to the guide provided, they found out what Hearst was all about. Spending vast sums of money on his castle in addition to millions for rare pictures, tapestries, sumptuous rooms, all kinds of bric-a-brac, and a fantastic swimming pool. Beautiful gardens, large dining rooms with great tables and grand chairs. Everything left you with a feeling of sadness for a man like Hearst, who could have spent more money on others, instead of feeding his ego acquiring precious treasures of all kinds and sizes.

No doubt he was without a peer, but he squelched and destroyed many people with his dictatorial attitude towards anyone who stood in his way.

• • •

San Francisco was the high point of the five week trip. For several days they made side trips from the city. Crossing the Oakland-Bay bridge and also the Golden Gate bridge.

Giant Sequoia trees made one feel intimidated to realize the hundreds of years they have withstood all kinds of atmospheric conditions.

Naturally, Fisherman's Wharf was checked out. Shops in the city were explored. Bob bought Maisie a beautiful Chinese figure that had a small part set aside for real flowers. It was over 50 years old.

• • •

Entering Nevada, the bus stopped for about 30 minutes at Reno and other cities. Maisie and Bob hit all the slots while in the state, especially in Las Vegas. Tallying up the results, they figured they picked up $35. At least they didn't lose their shirt as Bob boasted to Maisie.

Another highlight of the trip was a three day visit to Salt Lake City. Both of them had visited the small chapel built by the Mormons at the World's Fair in New York in 1930-1940.

First place to visit was the world famous Mormon Tabernacle. Guides explained that some sections of the Tabernacle were off limits except to the elders of the church. Mormons are expected to serve at least two years during their lifetime working in foreign missions.

During the Great Depression of the 1930's, they provided poor people all over the world with food and clothing. Bob was told that the Mormons provided what was needed for all their members without going on government assistance programs. Vast store houses, loaded with food, clothing and other basics were set up in many countries throughout the globe.

Maisie and Bob left Salt Lake City realizing what a great contribution Mormons had made to our country.

• • •

At Kansas City, they had a layover of 3 hours. Time was spent eating dinner and resting up. Next day they reached Chicago at 3 p.m. Since their bus was scheduled to leave at 10 a.m. the following day, several museums and big department stores were visited. Niagara Falls on both the United States and Canada sides were checked.

The next morning, Bob and Maisie arrived at the Newark Greyhound terminal and immediately switched to another

Greyhound and reported to their apartment on campus.

•   •   •

During his post-graduate work, at American University, Bob worked at Woodward and Lothrap part time. At least once a week he helped deliver merchandise to a Woodward and Lothrap store located in the Pentagon.

At the time there were over 25,000 persons (civilians and military) working there.

Bob often wondered who was minding the store. Regardless of the time of day, hundreds of customers were in all the specialty shops located in the central part of the building. The Defense Department was back to peace activity with a vengeance.

Many of the ex-servicemen were going to school on a very lean budget. Almost all of them, especially those with babies, constantly wrestled with short rations. At times Maisie would give food to those who had children. Everyone pitched in to help. All were in the same boat, trying to get a little more help.

•   •   •

During the first winter season at school, Bob read an article in the Post concerning the Red Cross. It seemed that it was the 75th birthday and they were going to hire 50 history students to write about their achievements. Each student was to be paid $10,000 for their part of the project. Bob applied and on being interviewed was asked which party he was registered in for voting purposes. He answered Republican. The interviewer told him to forget it since only Democrats were to be hired.

Bob was disgusted but he followed the aspiring historians through local news stories. Finally the booklet was finished. Since it was less then 50 pages, each person had contributed a page or less. It eventually cost over $10,000 per page.

• • •

At times, when the humidity was high, many of the ex G.I.s played croquet until 3 a.m. in the morning.

Maisie was employed in the campus cafeteria while Bob worked days in the Display Department at Woodward and Lothrap and attended classes at night. Often on a Sunday afternoon they took "Delilah Jane", an old Studebaker, purchased second hand from Maisie's boss, half way to Washington's home in Mt Vernon. There beside the Potomac, Bob studied and Maisie relaxed.

About every 2 months they took a trip to Newark to visit Maisie's relatives. In 2 years they had "Delilah Jane" konk out on them 4 times. However, the car always made it back to Washington. Bob used to "Call Kal" a group of service stations scattered throughout the city.

No sooner was one bill paid then another was added. It

seemed as if "Delilah Jane" had found a home.

Bob was taking classes at night. However, after 9 months he started to gather material for his doctorate. His thesis was to be "The National University Movement" (1789-1820)

Starting every day Monday through Friday he visited the National Archives. He had been given permission to examine the Journals of Congress. Each Journal was about 2'x3'.

He had to look at every page to make sure he picked up the information. It was tedious work. Often it wasn't always the best of writing.

However, in checking on the National University movement, Bob discovered some very pertinent information. Veterans of the Revolutionary War often petitioned Congress for pay they never received for service or trying to get Congress to pay their medical bills. It bothered Bob so much, he later checked out the War of 1812: Mexican War; Civil War; World War I and World War II.

Invariably Congress was quick to approve action, but then tended to forget the veterans.

Politics reared its ugly head, starting with John Adams and continued up until the present administration. Oftimes, instead of voting for the right bills that are non-partisan, it seems as if all our elected officials are only intent on personal self-interest. After their election they immediately start to pick the pockets of tax payers, but don't care how it affects our nation.

National Archives stored our historical information in ledgers when records were kept. Scholars must get permission to check the ledgers and must be careful since many of them are over 200 years old.

Often Bob worked continuously for 6 or 7 hours and then relaxed by visiting Congress while it was in session.

• • •

He was often in the Senate when Senator Bob Taft was at his desk, diligently working on committee projects. He seemed to be oblivious to everything unless another Senator asked for approval of some bill, at which time he requested a quorum to consider a vote. You could hear the bell ring and Senators strolled in until the chair recognized the sponsor of the proposed legislation. A vote was either taken or the sponsor withdrew his motion.

• • •

There are so many wind-bags; prevaricators; obnoxious partisans; dim-witted legislators; who care only about their own little fiefdom and consciously or unconsciously break down the fabric of our great nation.

Frankly, many citizens feel if they took off more time, we wouldn't get as much crazy legislation and the nation would be better served.

After spending hours and hours passing a bill only to discover hidden tidbits that bureaucrats use to change the bill, our legislators expect their constituents to rally behind their efforts.

Unless we eliminate lobbying by unions and other groups we will continue to get half-baked legislation that will only benefit the tort lawyers

• • •

Finally, Bob had concluded his work in the Archives Building and was busy assembling all he had discovered concerning the National University movement. Before he had completely finished, the president of the university asked several of the aspiring students to show him the results of their research.

Bob, feeling honored to be asked, quickly gave him everything, including all his notes. However, he made a tragic mistake. He didn't make any copies of his materials.

Several weeks later the president left the university with all their papers. No one seemed to know where he had gone. After a few months, Bob left the school hoping to get some information about him. Upon inquiring, he was told that he would have to do the research again or select another topic. He was thinking about another thesis, but decided that he wasn't going to spend another year of work.

Fifty years after he left the university, Bob wrote to the president and explained the situation and asked him what could be done. He was quickly informed that he must start all over. With that answer, Bob closed out the book on any chance for a doctorate in American History .

Chapter Eight

Teaching in Newark

Leaving American University in late 1950, Bob and Maisie rented a one room apartment on Lake Avenue.

Second stop in Ocean Grove was a third floor apartment on Mt. Herman Way. Renting from a blind man who loved the bottle, who continually entreated Bob to get him a fifth of Scotch. When delivered he went on another binge for a few days. Frankly, Bob enjoyed his company, especially when he was sober.

One of the problems facing anyone living in a sea shore community is that friends and relatives suddenly discover the urge to visit, especially over the weekend. Since Maisie only had a kitchen, bath and two bedrooms, it became crowded whenever adults often arrived simultaneously. Actually Maisie had four other married sisters, who often showed up. Sleeping on the floor, couch or bed required patience and stamina. Bob often took off for the beach to relax.

Maisie, on the other hand, spent most of her time providing topnotch meals for the company.

. . .

In March of 1951, they moved to a small house on Central Avenue. It had 2 small bedrooms, a tiny bath, a small living and dining area, plus a kitchen that must have been made for midgets. When the seasonal horde arrived, pandemonium hit a high level. You might say it really caused a stir.

Everyone spent most of the day on the beach. But when dinner was served the visitors often found themselves eating while sitting on the floor. However, all seemed to be enjoying themselves. "

Bob had applied for a teaching position in Asbury Park. Unfortunately, they had a full complement of teachers, who were receiving about $2,700 for the term. So, Bob hired out as a cashier in South Belmar in a local A& P store.

During his employment, he noticed one lady who continually bought lots of food for animals.

One day he remarked that she must have lots of pets.

"I'm buying that for my family. I found that if you mixed it with eggs its okay. Of course it's a little rough to eat."

Another incident occurred when he noticed a lady deliberately move a hand truck in the aisle and then fell down. She sued the company.. Bob told the insurance adjuster what happened.

"It was her own fault. She shouldn't get a penny."

Later he found out that she received $300.

"Why did you pay her $300?"

"It was cheaper to give her $300 instead of going to court. We saved the company money."

• • •

Later in the year, a new A & P store opened in Belmar. It was one of the first supermarkets.

Business was very brisk. Bob liked Fridays when the store was open from 7 a.m. until 9 p.m.

As a checker Bob had a spirited rivalry with John, another employee. Both checkers usually totaled over $4,000 for the day.

However, he had a problem with the manager. Whenever they had a spare minute the checkers worked on the shelves. One particular day stood out in Bob's mind. He was told to stock the shelves.

Before he finished with the first job, the manager gave him a second order. He was still working on the first part when he spotted the manager coming down the aisle. He immediately started to take cans off the shelves and put them in a case on the floor.

"What are you doing? Why aren't you stocking?" He was yelling and his face was flushed.

"You've given me two extra details and now you intend to add another job.
Either you stop hounding me or I'm walking out the door."

After the outburst, the manager turned and walked away. Needless to say, he never bothered Bob again.

In June he had taken a written and oral test for a teaching position in Newark, the state's largest city. Coming in 16th out of 300 applicants, he was hired as a teacher and was assigned to Morton Street School.

Near the end of August, he resigned from the supermarket and prepared to enter the teaching profession.

• • •

Starting the first day of school, Bob was assigned the 7th Grade with 51 students. Several students had to sit on chairs.

During the morning session he explained to the students what he expected them to accomplish by the end of the term. His motto "Nothing for Nothing" was placed on the blackboard, where it remained for the entire term.

The school day was divided into 8 periods. During the week the girls and boys had physical education on alternate days. At other periods, the girls went to cooking class, with the boys going to industrial arts.

It became obvious that some of the students were not working on the grade level. Some remedial work had to be done. Bob found that it was necessary to repeat lessons until it finally made an impression.

Spelling consumed a lot of time. It was necessary to break down the words so they understood what they meant.

In mathematics, review was consistently made on multiplication, addition and subtraction to bring everyone up to grade level.

English was taught in addition to spelling. Sentence structure was very important. Reading was essentially tied in with most other subjects.

• • •

Communism was being pushed by the local establishment during the Eisenhower years. Newspapers were featuring anti-American programs. Bob felt that our high schools should explain to students what the Russians really were trying to accomplish. So he wrote a letter to the Newark Superintendent of Schools. He urged him to add to the high school curriculum a course spotlighting the real aims of the Red dictatorship.

Previously the downtown establishment had discontinued the Industrial Arts program. So Bob rescued four worktables and a few tools and placed them in his room. After adding a few hammers, saws, lumber and nails he started the boys on a light program of making small tables, bookends, birdhouses and other small objects. While the girls were in gym, the period was spent trying to help the students finish items that made them proud of their own work.

One day, as the boys were working on their projects, the Assistant Superintendent of Schools walked in the room. Although Bob saw him, he waited until the period was over and then talked with him. He was informed that the Superintendent didn't think it was a good idea to add a course in the high school explaining things about the Russian leaders. Two years later they started an identical program, Bob was then informed that he would have to stop his Industrial Arts activity. Since the boys were using saws and hammers, they might cut and hurt themselves, and they could sue the Board of Education.

• • •

Teaching at Morton Street changed over the 22 years Bob was there. Usually he had 40 to 50 students until the last four years. Starting with almost 2,000 students and with 31 teachers, the school had about 1,000 with 65 teachers by the late 1970s. Average class size was about 27.

When he started in 1952, there was no discipline. If a problem arose, you sent the student to the principal's office and it was taken in hand. During the desegregation era there was much hostility between the teachers. Sixty-five percent of the children were black and the rest were Hispanic.

By 1970 parents and students were blasting the teachers.

Activists were attempting to get control of the schools. Principals and vice principals were often intimidated.

One year a directive was sent to all schools that teachers should strive for 100% promotion. In March a questionnaire was sent to all teachers to find out the status of promotion. Bob was the last one to get the paper and he checked and discovered that all students in Morton Street were to be promoted. He wrote 82% for his class. Within 10 minutes he was called to the principal's office.

"Why haven't you listed 100%. Every teacher but you has done so?"

"Excuse me, I'm going to get my papers."

Returning Bob turned test papers over to the principal. Bob wrote, not promoted and signed them.

"I can't pass these five students. None of the papers is even near a passing grade. Besides they're two grades behind in English, Arithmetic, Social Studies and other courses. I'm not going to mark promotion on their report cards. I'll send the cards to you in June and you can sign them." The principal didn't sign them.

On opening day of the new school year, Bob arrived early and saw the five students on the playground.

"What did you do, go to summer school?"

"Oh no. The principal said we didn't have to go."

As soon as Bob entered the office he inquired about the students.

"Why did the five students get promoted?"

"Well, they went to summer school."

"Don't lie to me. They told me that you said they didn't need to attend summer school."

With that statement, Bob walked out. He lost all respect for the principal. It was the beginning of the end for his teaching position.

· · ·

In the early 70's Bob noticed that each year more Hispanics entered Morton Street. So he decided to do something about helping them to speak better English.

Spending his own money, he bought a series of lessons from the Berlitz Company. For a period of three years, he had any students who wanted help, meet him from 8 a.m. until 8:30 a.m., on Monday, Wednesday, and Friday mornings. At times there were 10 to 20 students each day. Finally, someone blew the whistle at downtown headquarters and Bob was politely informed that he had to stop the program, because it wasn't authorized by the establishment.

"I guess I must be considered a maverick. All I ever wanted to do was help the students," Bob later explained to Maisie.

· · ·

Over the years several changes were made that directly hurt the school system.

First and foremost was the introduction into the curriculum of the New Math. All the teachers were indoctrinated with the idea that they were going to help the students. Bob never bought the ideas and he decided he would not teach it.

New Math was so bad, that most of the teachers couldn't understand it themselves, Bob's class continued to get the basics, such as the multiplication tables, addition and subtraction problems. Repeating many times, until at least the students eventually could function as students who could get a job in the real world.

Without a doubt, New Math was, foisted on the schools by looney professors and under-handed school administrators.

• • •

In March 1974, Bob was conducting a Reading Class. All of a sudden, one of the larger boys stood up.

"Will you please sit down." Twice repeated.

"No, I don't have to."

Bob, while having the reading class continue, walked slowly over to the student and put him down in his seat.

After leaving the student, Bob walked to the other side of

the room.

Immediately, he stood up again.

"Will you please sit down.'" Twice repeated.

"No, you can't make me."

Bob walked to the boy and pushed him down again.

He was no sooner on the other side of the room, when the student stood up. Bob, realizing he had reached the end of his patience, decided to send him to the front office.

"Go down to the principal's office, tell him what you were doing and that I want to see your parents. In addition, you are to apologize to the class for stubbornly refusing to sit down."

"I'm not going."

Bob slowly walked to the student. Seeing the boy holding both hands on the desk he used his left arm to pull him from his seat.

Leaving the room, he almost carried him down four flights of steps until he reached the office. By the time he reached the office, Bob had become exhausted.

Dropping the boy on a chair, he explained to the principal that he wanted to see the boys' mother and he insisted on an apology to the class.

While in the cafeteria, he again explained what had happened.

In the afternoon he checked the class, and was disturbed to find the student sitting in his chair with a big smile on his face.

"I thought you were told to get your mother and to apologize to the class."

"The principal sent me back."

Immediately, Bob got his neighboring teacher to watch his class and hurried to the office.

"Didn't I explain what I wanted him to do?"

"I couldn't do that. We're in the midst of integration. It's impossible."

"Is that your final decision?"

Hearing the principal's decision, Bob returned to his room.

Returning home, Bob explained to Maisie what had happened.

"What do you think I should do?"

"Well, whatever you decide is okay with me."

"I want to resign. For the last three years I've been frustrated. Discipline is non-existent.

However if I resign, I'll lose one half of my pension. That will mean losing thousands of dollars. Frankly if I stay in Newark teaching, sooner or later I'm afraid I'll lose my temper and might lose all my pension.

"Money isn't everything. I've more or less thought that peace of mind is more important."

The next day Bob tendered his resignation to the principal, effective at the end of term.

Chapter Nine

First Adoption

"We sincerely regret that we must inform you of our inability to accept your application. Our agency already has a large number of families approved and waiting for a toddler of the type which you discussed during your intake interview. We believe your waiting period with this agency, would therefore be of such length, that it would not be productive for your family's needs."

Seven years have passed since Maisie and Bob first talked about the feasibility of adopting a little girl, preferably between the ages of three months and three years. Their latest letter of rejection, of which an excerpt is printed above, is merely one more road block in the path leading to the goal that they have set for themselves.

Reviewing events of the past few years, they recall vividly many heartaches and disappointments. It is because of these experiences that the article was written. Perhaps, in the retelling, it may help other prospective parents to understand many of the problems involved in child placement.

After an intense period of checking with numerous agencies, it was felt that their best chances for adoption lay with a children's home agency located in a nearby city. Once their minds were synchronized, arrangements were made with the supervisor of the agency. A formal interview was scheduled for Christmas week in 1952.

During this meeting a brief orientation was given concerning the responsibilities and financial obligations of the organization. Both learned that all children, under supervision of the agency, were left in foster homes until they were permanently placed with an adoptive family. Periodic tests, although by no means infallible, provided a guide to the children's future growth and development. Each child costs the agency an average of about $1000. However, adoptive parents pay only a certain percentage, based upon their annual income.

Upon returning home, they completed a formal application form which had been given to them at the intake interview. Questions concerning their financial status, religious affiliation and ancestry were answered. Reports on their physical examinations, including a statement of sterility were also sent.

Nothing further was heard from the agency's representative until July. At that time a letter arrived informing them that the application had not been studied and would not likely be considered for several more months. Eventually instructions were sent telling them to call at the agency in December. After arrival at the agency, both were subjected to a concentrated interview. Information bearing upon the application form was discussed.

Individual interviews were scheduled in January and February. Maisie and Bob were each given thorough interrogations. Physical and emotional factors that were involved in the prospective adoption were weighed very carefully by the case worker as she questioned them. Statements made in previous interviews were checked and rechecked for accuracy. However, they always told them the truth, even though it did not always place them in the most favorable light. ·

Following the individual conferences, an appointment was made for the purpose of inspection of their home. After checking it, the inspector decided that the yard area was too small. This, in spite of the fact, that the play area measured twenty-five feet by seven feet.

Prospects for successful adoption of an infant appeared to be dimming. To be rejected because of inadequate play space would indeed be ironic. But they had done all that it was possible to do.

Within the next few weeks all references were contacted. While discussing the case with their minister, the investigator mentioned the small yard as a possible reason for the rejection of their application. Fortunately, the minister was able to checkmate such a possibility by explaining to the case worker that he had raised a son and a daughter in an apartment house.

Maisie and Bob's application was approved by the agency's board.

Several hectic weeks passed. A baby's room was newly

painted and papered. A crib, mattress, bureau and many small baby toys were purchased. Clothing, appropriate for a baby girl, was stocked pending the new arrival.

Suddenly all of their well laid plans were completely upset. Word arrived from the agency supervisor that they had an older boy available for adoption. After prolonged discussion, they contacted the agency and learned that the child was three and one-half years of age. Deciding to investigate further an appointment was made in early April.

According to the information supplied, Jack had never been accepted by his real mother. She had placed him with her sister as an infant. Within a year the sister was divorced and Jack was shoved around to various neighbors. Finally, an elderly couple (near 65) took him into their home. He had been living with them for nine months. Maisie and Bob agreed to take Jack provided acceptance would not interfere with later placement of a little girl. An acute situation had developed since Jack's foster mother was scheduled for a major operation in 3 weeks. Therefore, it was necessary to make an immediate placement.

The case worker revealed that they had been under consideration as the prospective parents for about six weeks. In fact, she had been conditioning Jack to the acceptance of a new mommy and daddy for several weeks, and to make it easier for him he was shown their pictures.

Arrangements were completed to take Jack on a picnic the following Wednesday. If everything went all right, they were to invite him to their home for the weekend. Arriving at the headquarters building, Jack greeted them by presenting Maisie with a rose and gave Bob a cigar and within a few moments everyone became very friendly. Leaving the office all drove to a local park located a few blocks away. While there, Jack visited a small zoo. He was given several kiddie rides and they gave him a hot dog, soda, ice cream and candy. After two hours had passed all returned to the agency.

During the course of the picnic, Maisie invited their prospective son to spend the weekend with them. One condition was thoroughly understood, that at any time he felt like it, they would return him to his foster home. In case he decided to remain, he would not be returned at all, but stay with them permanently.

Friday afternoon, Jack was met, accompanied by the state case worker, at one of the many traffic circles. He had on high topped shoes and old fashioned clothing. His hair cut made him look as if he had just stepped out of another era. Everything he had was in a small box which was transferred to their car. The first thing he said was that he expected to stay only a few days. They agreed and told him that any time he wanted to go back to his "old home" they would take him.

Discovering he was near tears, Maisie asked him if he felt like visiting a big city.

He agreed, and they started on their way. Reaching the city, all proceeded to the largest department store and visited the toy section. Their son picked out the largest gun he could find, twice as big as he was. For the next few minutes he stood in the main aisle of the store, shooting everyone in sight with a wide grin on his face. Observing that he seemed to be tiring, Bob headed for home. On the way he fell asleep. Upon awaking, several miles from their house, he started asking questions concerning his "new home."

At last, the big moment arrived. Their son was home. His arrival was something quite different than they had planned, since they had expected a baby girl. Questions popped from Jack as he made a tour of inspection. His room pleased him immensely, especially when he noticed the boats, sailors and maps that made up the design of his wallpaper.

At five o'clock a very light supper was served. Jack wasn't too hungry. That was understandable, since he had been stuffing himself all afternoon on hot dogs, candy, peanuts and soda. About seven-thirty their son was shown to his room and daddy started a Bible story which had to be continued the next night because he fell asleep in the middle of it.

Maisie and Bob returned to the living room and started to discuss Jack's arrival.

One thing was very clear, their orderly routine had to go. In the beginning a lively child had been requested. That was one request that the agency certainly filled with a vengeance.

Saturday morning dawned bright and clear. At seven o'clock everyone was up preparing for their first full day together as a family. In a few moments Jack came downstairs and took his place at the table. The first thing he said was that he intended to stay with them and he wasn't going back to his "old home" again. Jack's adjustment was remarkable. Accepting as perfectly natural a mother-father relationship he immediately faced up to his altered status. Their adjustment was somewhat longer, but with their son's help they made it within a few weeks.

Maisie had the most difficult adjustment to make. Preparing for a little girl, a point on which she had set her heart, accepting Jack who wasn't a baby, but was already on his own, and then being told repeatedly by Jack that he didn't like girls made her task indeed formidable.

Many times their son had mentioned a diner in which he had evidently spent a great amount of time with a man he called Uncle Jim. Uncle Jim made such a lasting impression on him that he talked about him for several months. Often he asked to eat in diners, and even now he mentions how nice it is to eat in a diner.

Inability to play with his toys for any length of time was the first problem they had with Jack. If sent out to play, he usually developed an excuse to get back into the house. It was also hard for him to play with his playmates for even a short period.

After much discussion it was decided that his background played an important part in his inability to concentrate on normal play activities. Since he had been raised around older folks, he acted more serious. In fact, his choice of words was so good for his age level that he often flabbergasted their friends and relatives.

Unfortunately, many mistakes were made in meeting the problems posed by Jack's arrival. At first they attempted to smother him with gifts and affection. Of course he reacted against it. His toys were largely ignored, nothing seemed to affect him. However, that was due to their indulgence.

Christmas, the first year with Jack was a complete flop. A

train outfit was bought and of course they couldn't wait for Christmas, starting to set up the tracks in late November.

Their Christmas tree was decorated a week before the holiday. When the big day finally dawned, all the excitement was gone. After a number of rebuffs it finally dawned on them that they were responsible for their son's peculiar actions. Both decided to stop providing him with what they wanted him to have.

Several weeks after Jack's arrival, he was left in the cellar to play. Realizing that he had become exceptionally quiet, Maisie investigated. She discovered that he had been redecorating both the cellar and himself His clothes were ruined, and he had paint all over his face and hands. The cellar looked as if a surrealistic painter had gone on a binge. Actually, it was their fault for leaving the paint within reach. Another expensive lesson was learned the hard way.

Right from the start, everything was explained to Jack about his coming adoption.

The story always started with their picking him out as their little boy because he was wanted.

Naturally, he was informed that it would be necessary for them to go to court at the end of the first year and make his adoption legal.

After four months of being with them Jack came to Bob and asked if he would take him on an airplane ride on the day he became "our boy". Once it was agreed, he became very happy and was continually reminding them that he expected to pilot the plane.

Adoption Day finally arrived. Maisie and Bob went to the court house where they waited two hours before a judge called them into his chamber. Final approval was a mere formality, because the executive director of the agency had already briefed him. Both were sworn in and talked with the judge for only a few moments. He signed the papers and the hearing was officially over.

The first order of business upon returning home was to tell Jack all about the formal adoption. After lunch Bob went to the airport where Jack took his first airplane ride. The pilot let him handle the stick for a few minutes. Before it even landed, Jack had extracted a promise from Bob to take him up once again.

Several years have passed since Jack entered their family. Many problems have been met and overcome. Each day brings its problems and rewards.

When Jack was twelve, he used to take off. One day he disappeared at eight in the morning. After Bob had spent most of the day and evening looking for him, they decided to call the police. At that moment, Jack strolled into the house.

"Where have you been? We've been looking all day for you."

"Oh, I just decided to walk to Freehold. I lost track of time"

"Well, don't go out again unless you let us know."

This was the start of Jack's escapades. Over the next 3 years, he would take off on 10 more junkets.

First stop was South Carolina. Just as he did in all his adventures, he hitch-hiked with tractor trailer drivers. Next stop was Virginia, followed by another trip to South Carolina, but the police always picked him up.

It always seemed that Bob received a call about Jack after midnight. Bob would start out and often drive for 12 to 14 hours, depending on where Jack had finally stopped running.

Once, when Bob picked him up in North Carolina, he explained that he was in jail and could easily have escaped, since the wood around the bars was rotten. Bob told him that would have been the wrong thing to do.

One day he took off at noon. Bob figured out that he had caught a bus to New York. Going to the Asbury Greyhound station, he discovered Jack had purchased a ticket. The station master called New York and told them to hold him until Bob picked him up.

However, Jack left the bus at Woodbridge. Once again he hitched a ride with a truck driver. A week later Bob received a call from the police in Fairfax to collect his son.

One night, about 1:00 a.m., Bob had a call from the Chief of Police in Myrtle Beach. When he arrived the next day, he talked to the Chief. It seems that Jack had been sleeping under the boardwalk. When they picked him up he had a big bunch of keys in his pocket.

Unfortunately the keys belonged to an automobile dealer

who had lost several cars in a recent robbery. Jack insisted that he had found the keys along the highway. Besides, he insisted that he had been staying with a family in town. However, he refused to tell the police who it was since he didn't want to get the family in trouble.

Bob told Jack he better tell the police, since the Chief had told him if he didn't, he was going to be held for the local judge. The judge would throw Jack in jail as a juvenile and he wouldn't get out until he was eighteen.

So finally Jack took the Chief to the home where he had been staying. Jack knocked on the door and as soon as the door opened, the lady recognized him.

"Hi, Jack, how are you?"

The Police Chief was satisfied. Returning to his office he released Jack. Bob immediately started for New Jersey and they arrived home at 3:00 a.m.

Bob, by this time, was slowly burning up. He told Maisie the next time he wasn't going to go after Jack.

Two months later Jack was picked up by the Cleveland police. Bob talked to the Chief and asked him to see that Jack was placed aboard a plane for Newark. One of Bob's friends went with him to bring Jack home. During the trip back, Jack raved about the wonderful way they treated him.

When Bob got home, he told Maisie how pleased Jack was about the trip.

"The only thing that I'm concerned about during all these episodes is that even though Jack is often thrown in jail, he's never used any drugs. At least he remembers what I've always emphasized about the dangers involved."

Later Jack met a girl, who already had a son, fell in love and married at eighteen.

He left home and proceeded to work as a tractor trailer driver as soon as he qualified.

Chapter Ten

Second Adoption

Four years have passed since Maisie and Bob adopted Jack. For two years they waited for a baby girl. The agency had a long list of persons interested in adopting a girl.

On a visit to Marietta, Bob had a chance to talk to his former doctor. He informed Bob that one of his patients was a girl, who was six months into her pregnancy, and was anxious to give the baby, when born, to any couple who would pay all the expenses, including the physician and hospital bills.

Maisie and Bob discussed the proposal.

"Frankly, I don't think there's much chance of our receiving a girl from the agency. They don't give us very much encouragement."

"Don't forget Maisie we have no idea whether it's a boy or a girl."

"I'm tired of waiting. I will take the responsibility, if you agree."

"All right, I'll inform Dr. Jason that we will assume all expenses. He can call us when she is admitted to St. Joseph's Hospital."

Returning to Ocean Grove Maisie and Bob eagerly awaited a call from Dr. Jason.

At last they received word that Hannah gave birth to a boy. However, since it was a premature birth, he would be kept in the intensive care unit for at least five weeks.

Several trips were made to St. Joseph's at which time arrangements were made to pay the physician and the hospital.

At last they were informed that Dennis was to be picked up. Arriving in Lancaster, it was necessary to sign papers with the state of Pennsylvania since he was going to New Jersey. Arriving in Ocean Grove, documents were filed in Trenton.

For twelve months representatives visited the home regularly to make sure that they were providing adequate care for their son.

Arriving home on Wednesday afternoon, Dennis was immediately accepted as his brother by Jack. Over the years, Dennis always had a great relationship and affection for his older brother.

One Friday afternoon, Dennis became very sick and was taken to Fitkin Hospital, where he remained for six weeks. Maisie and Bob were very concerned about the contraptions that were attached to his head. Dr. Desmond informed them that they were monitoring his brain and other organs.

At last he was discharged and Dennis was sent home. During the entire first year, he was returned to the hospital off and on for stays of from one day to over a week. During this period of time, Dennis was given all kinds of medication. Finally after one year had passed, he was stabilized. Medication costs for the year averaged $25.00 per week, without including hospital costs. Maisie and Bob thanked Dr. Desmond for his great work.

Actually, the doctor informed them he never did know what had solved the problem. Evidently he had finally hit the correct formula. However, Maisie and Bob felt the many prayers that were made by them and many friends certainly made a difference.

When Dennis reached his first birthday, Judge Gage signed the adoption papers, legalizing the adoption.

Incidentally, a month before the Judge approved the adoption, the agency sent word that they had a baby girl for them. Naturally, they decided against it, since there was always a chance that Dennis' problems might return.

Because of his sickness, Maisie spoiled Dennis outrageously. As he got older, he often took advantage of her concern.

Having decided on a little girl, and then accepting another son, she put most of her love and attention on her young son. Jack never seemed to mind and since he was four when adopted, he had developed a life long attitude that nothing would ever bother him. Having been in several foster homes he accepted anything with no fuss and moved on with his life.

Dr. Desmond had told Maisie and Bob that Dennis would be at least a year in back of his classmates. That certainly was very true. So they asked the doctor if he would take care of him until he reached 14, which he did.

At four years of age, Dennis was riding his bicycle in front of the house, when the chain stopped moving. Getting off his bike, he somehow got his right index finger caught in the chain. It removed part of his finger and he was rushed to the hospital where Dr. Locke, a specialist, operated on it. He grafted a piece of skin from Dennis' leg. However, the tip of the finger was lost.

For the rest of his life, he was definitely conscious of the deformity. Often other playmates ridiculed him. (Children are often unaware of hurting feelings.) Starting school in September of 1962, Dennis was enrolled in the Ocean Grove Elementary School. Right from the start, he had a difficult time trying to keep up with his classmates. In April as he was finishing the third grade, Bob visited the teacher and principal.

He explained to them since he was born prematurely, he would tend to be a trifle slower at learning, than his classmates.

Bob suggested that he be retained in the third grade for another year. However, they passed him anyhow. (Actually, they were concerned with 100% promotion.)

After a month in the fourth grade, they realized their mistake and sent him back to the third grade. Maisie and Bob were outraged and let the administration know how they felt.

However, the damage was done.

Dennis, in addition to the taunts about his finger, had to endure jeers about his being demoted. He never forgot it.

Any enthusiasm he had about school was crushed. No longer would he think of school as a place he cared about. He played hooky often staying in an old shed next to Days.

Sometimes he was discovered lying under the boardwalk. Often he was picked up by the police in other towns.

After school Dennis and his friends would play in the park at the entrance to Broadway. Once they decided to start a fire. Gathering paper and wood, they put a match to it.

However, one of the neighbors called the police. She also called Maisie.

Maisie drove to the park just in time to see the three urchins get in the police cruiser. She followed. Looking out the back window, they saw her and started waving and smiling. It's a good thing Maisie couldn't get at them. She might have lost her cool.

Arriving at the office, they were plunked on chairs, and each individually taken into the Chiefs office. He acted very serious and gave them a severe tongue lashing. Later, Maisie took Dennis home and explained how serious it was to play with matches and what could happen if it started a big fire.

Once their big overgrown dog, Buster, broke loose and was picked up by the police. Maisie was called and she sent Dennis to pick him up. However, he forgot the dog's chain. So putting his arm around Buster, he literally dragged him home. Dennis was so exhausted that he stopped at a neighbor's home and borrowed a strong rope which he tied around the dog's neck Dennis finally reached home.

During the thirteen years Maisie and Bob operated Days, Dennis was a great help.

For a short time, he operated the dishwasher. Next he collected all the dishes as a bus boy. With over 200 chairs, it was necessary to hire others to help. On busy days it was necessary to have at least 3 boys.

After 4 years, Bob put Dennis in charge of desserts. That included apple cobbler, rice pudding, jello, layer cake, lemon chiffon and other pies, in addition to preparing all kinds of sodas and sundaes. Each year, in addition to his weekly salary, Bob put $500 in a savings account for his son.

Dennis kept the waitresses on their toes. If he made up a sundae, it was supposed to be picked up at once. If it started to look mushy he would send word to the girls. At times they were a little agitated but they usually cooperated.

Each year in August, in honor of Dennis' birthday all the employees were taken to Perkins Restaurant by Bob. Everyone ordered whatever they wanted. It was always a fun time for all.

Dennis was always appreciative of any gifts he received from Maisie and Bob. It was quite a contrast for them, since Jack had never shown much of an interest in anything he was given. In many ways they differed but they both really had a good relationship and very rarely ever had any arguments.

Chapter Eleven

DAYS

Maisie and Bob had often talked about the possibility of purchasing Days Restaurant and Ice Cream Garden.

However, in May of 1962, they had an opportunity to buy the Wedgewood restaurant on Main Street. The purchase price was $45,000.

Maisie, who helped Helen and Henry, the owner of Days Restaurant, asked her employers what they thought of buying the Wedgewood. Both thought the price was too high.

"Why don't you wait a few years and you can buy Days? We'll be ready to retire and we know you can think about it." Maisie and Bob decided to wait awhile.

In May of 1963, a former restaurateur from New York City made Helen and Henry an offer they couldn't refuse. So they sold Days for over three times as much money as they had paid for it in 1950.

Naturally, Maisie and Bob were disappointed, but they decided to invest in some real estate. They purchased a 2 family house on Franklin Avenue. They moved Maisie's sister and her husband into one section and rented out the second apartment.

A few years later they had an opportunity to buy The Sport Shoppe on Main Avenue. A small down payment was made and they opened in June 1935. It was a summer operation, open four months, from June through September. It was an ideal setup, since Bob was available during his summer vacation. Maisie prepared all the meals and Bob handled the supplies and paid the staff.

Breakfast, lunch and dinner were served along with ice cream after dinner. Eight tables alongside both walls provided seating for 32 customers. At the back of the room was a counter and restaurant equipment.

Waitresses placed tickets on the counter and picked up their orders in regular rotation. The Sports Shoppe was operated for three summers with increased business each year.

On the 27th of December, 1967, Bob met Bronson, a local realtor. "Do you know anything about Days being for sale? I'd like to buy it. I know the owner died in October."

"You're in luck. His sister, the executor of his estate, placed it with us to sell."

"Okay, I'll buy it. Here's a check for $1,000 as a down payment. I'll have the rest of the money by March 10, 1968."

Hurrying home, Bob broke the news to Maisie, who was very happy.

"It's a dream come true. I've wanted Days for years."

"We'll have to raise $45,000 before March 10th. I'll have to check and see if we can sell The Sports Shoppe, our home at 102 Lawrence and the duplex at 125 Franklin Avenue."
"The seller will take a first mortgage for $35,000. That leaves us $10,000 short.

Maybe we can sell all the properties and get the other $10,000. We have heavy mortgages on all three properties."

January and February passed and nobody was interested in buying any of the three properties.
On March 3rd, Bob decided to ask Helen and Henry if they wished to take a second mortgage for $10,000 with 10% interest being charged.

Since they had owned Days from 1950 to 1963, they readily agreed. Besides Maisie had worked for them for 6 years during the summer season.

On March 10th, Maisie and Bob moved into Days and started preparing for the opening on June 10th. Bob realized what a big project they had undertaken. So he started a proof-reading position at the Newark Star Ledger.

Once Henry, who was helping Bob the first year, was pre-paring 30 gallons of homemade clam chowder. The store was right under a skylight. At the same time Dennis and friends were playing war on the roof with several hundred plastic and tin soldiers. As they were conducting their war games, several figures plopped into the soup. Henry was stirring the soup and found soldiers.

"Bob, get your son to stop. He's ruining my soup. If you don't stop him, I'm walking out the door."

With his face a fiery red and brandishing his big spoon, it was evident that he meant what he said. So Bob moved Dennis and his friends to another part of the roof.

During the period from 1968 through 1973, Bob was paying first and second mortgages on Days and first mortgages on the Lawrence and Franklin Avenue properties.

Actually, he took a loss on all three properties. However, Bob was happy to get rid of the payments. He also finished off the second mortgage on Days in three years.

Maisie and Bob were very fortunate during the first season. Over 5,000 Quakers held their convention in the Great Auditorium. Many of them ate their meals throughout their convention week at Days.

At night, about 9:30, they finished their deliberations and came to Days for home made ice cream. It seemed like the rain poured down every night. But everyone was well satisfied with the work of the convention. It was often 1:00 a.m. before they left, but Bob enjoyed every minute because of the congeniality of the Quakers. All the hotels, restaurants and businesses had a very profitable week.

Bob had quite a schedule drawn up for himself during the

year. He usually left at 6:15 a.m. for Newark. Finishing teaching at 3:15, Bob walked to the Star-Ledger building and worked from 4 to 12. Leaving at midnight he caught a North Jersey train at 12:45 and arrived home at 3 a.m.

Sleeping from 3:15 to 6:15, he caught the train to Newark, arriving in time to teach at Morton Street about 8:15. This arrangement lasted for 10 years.

In Newark, he taught his class from Monday thru Friday. At the Star Ledger, he worked Friday through Tuesday. During the summer vacation, he was replaced at the Star-Ledger with a substitute union member.

Opening in June 1968, Maisie and Bob went on a roller coaster ride of great adventure. Although she had a solid back ground in restaurant activity, he was like a man bailing for dear life in a sinking boat.

Fortunately, she took over the hostess duties and Henry supervised the kitchen. Henry drew up the daily menu and helped the chef. Albert, a refined black man, did all the cooking, with some help from two high school students.

Each day a daily special was featured. Sandwiches were prepared to order, with several special hot items. For example, broiled flounder with lemon sauce was featured Monday thru Saturday. Special of the day cost $2.95. Lunch, which was served from 11:30 a.m. until 2:00 p.m., featured 4 different salad bowls. Usually they had a full house. Since they had over 200 chairs in the garden, it put a heavy pressure on the kitchen help to keep things moving smoothly.

Dinner always listed five basic items including lamb, pot roast, baked chicken, filet mignon and blue fish. In addition, a special item was offered for $4.95. It included beverage and dessert.

Mornings were spent purchasing special items, and preparing for lunch and dinner.

Albert, the chef, was an excellent cook. He was employed six days, with Monday off. However, after receiving his pay, he spent the entire day hitting the bottle.

Unfortunately, he had too many friends and he usually reported for work on Tuesday completely broke. Al stayed at Days for two summers and then took off for greener pastures.

Walt, our third year cook, had to be called when lunch and dinner was served. Frankly, he was a pain in the butt and was always looking for an excuse to claim discrimination.

Bob made a serious mistake in hiring Joe as chef for the fourth year. When hired, he asked if there were other black people working. Although he himself was black, he informed Bob that he couldn't work with members of his own race. He was politely informed that no one discriminated against anyone at Days. So he agreed to the terms.

Joe started working. He was a sad sack as a chef. He usually spent one day making clam chowder for the week. Part of another day he prepared home-made dressing. In the mean time, Bob was roasting and preparing meals. Joe hardly ever served on the steam table. So Bob and two young helpers filled all the orders for dinner. Besides his sluggish work, Joe was talking to himself about the waitresses discriminating against him.

Finally, Bob had enough of his complaints. He called Joe into another room and sounded off.

"You told me that you couldn't work with your own people. Now you're accusing the girls of ignoring you. I'm tired of hearing your guff. Do you see that door?

If you're not satisfied quit and take off. I don't care if it's the middle of August. We'll do all right if you go. Otherwise, keep your mouth shut and do the work you are being paid for." Not another complaint was ever made.

Alan, who made all the ice cream for Days, was picked on by one of the waitresses. He never said anything about discrimination but one of the girls informed Bob.

He called her into the tea room.

"Did you say something to Al?"

"Yes, I did."

"Go up to the counter. You're fired. I'll give you your money. You should apologize for talking that way."

Opening the next year, the girl applied for a waitress position.
"You have to see Alan. If he accepts your apology and doesn't mind if you are hired it will be okay."

Never again did she step out of line. Alan was a complete gentleman. Not many would have acted as gentlemanly.

Another year a convention of about 6,000 Brethren were conducting services in the auditorium for a week. Like religious conventions all of the participants seemed to be re-charging their batteries to return home for greater Christian fellowship. It certainly was a high point for the season in Ocean Grove.

Saturday nights were usually very hectic after the programs ended in the Auditorium about 9:30. People piled into the garden. After all the seats were taken there would be many more waiting in line to finally come in.

Bob usually didn't open the back tea room. One night he seated 60 extra people there. However, he had 2 waitresses take their orders. All the orders for 60 people were taken before they were placed at the bottom of the pile. That meant the customers in the tea room were going to be served last.

After 30 minutes, half of the customers walked out, followed by others. By the time the girls brought the ice cream specialties, there were only 10 persons left. The help managed to take care of the extras. Bob learned his lesson well. Never again did he open the tea room for ice cream.

Starting with 12 girls on Saturday nights, Bob cut back to six. Each girl was assigned a specific section. Orders were taken from only one table at a time.

Bob also realized that people had to be recognized. He carried pitchers of ice water to the tables. Each section was served according to the time it was received. Since customers were served in correct order very few walked out.

For eight straight years the highlight of the season in June was the Institute sponsored by Bill Gothard. Monday through Thursday it was in session from 7:00 p.m. to 10 p.m. Friday opened at 9:00 a.m. and finished at 8:p.m. Saturday hours closed at 6:00 p.m.

From Monday through Thursday those who signed for the sessions in the Great Auditorium arrived early and many stopped at Days first. About 8:30 many also came over on a 15 minute break.

On Friday they had a break in the morning; lunch period for an hour; break in the afternoon; dinner around 5: 00 p.m. and a final break in the evening. Saturday was similar to Friday's schedule.

All the participants in the Institute paid a fee of $55. That allowed them to attend all meetings. In addition they received a large notebook in which they could write down all pertinent information. Bill Gothard was visible on one screen while all the salient points were written on another screen. Institute members diligently copied everything of interest to them.

Although it was aimed specifically at younger members to explain how everyone should approach life's problems, it also covered older individuals.

It was a great sight to see members seeking enlightenment and working together to provide strong family life.

During the entire week the Institute members rushed over to Days where they were directed to the kitchen. Sandwiches were available, pies, cake and ice cream were already on the counter. Hot items were served from the stove. Filling their trays, they emerged from the kitchen. Bob sat at a table and received the money. Coffee and tea were outside in the garden. Everyone helped themselves. At times it was necessary for him to check the kitchen. He would leave the table with several hundred dollars on it and move away.

One day one of the tourists who had been watching the operation talked to Bob.

"Aren't you afraid someone might walk off with the money? I'm a Captain with the New York Police Department."

"Well, this isn't New York. I've never lost a dime. Ocean Grove is a wonderful town. The mission of the Camp Meeting is to provide a place for rest, relaxation, and religion. It's a place to visit, relax and go home, with a renewed spirit to finish the rest of the year."

Since Days made their own ice cream, state inspectors diligently inspected the restaurant each year. During the fourth year's inspection, they found 25 violations.

"We're going to close the restaurant."

"What can I do so we can re-open?"

"We'll return in the morning. However, I don't believe you will take care of everything by 10:00 a.m."

"Okay. We'll be ready for you."

Bob recruited 15 workers. Starting at 6:00 p.m. they worked

through the night until 6:00 a.m. Every piece of equipment was cleaned. All dishes were run through the dishwasher. Loose paint was removed and part of the restaurant was repainted. Floors and walls were cleaned. At 6:00 a.m. everything was finished. Everyone was given a hearty breakfast and returned home to sleep for a few hours. Bob started preparing for the lunch hour starting at 11: 00 a.m.

At 10:00 a.m. the inspection crew returned. All 25 violations had been corrected. There were 4 men checking everything. Two inspectors were from the state and another local inspector. About 10:30, Dr. Watkins, the chief inspector strolled in.

"How many inspectors are working for the state?"

"Twenty-nine are in my department."

"My, my, Days must be very important. We have 10% of your entire work force here."

After finishing the inspections, they handed Bob a paper with 12 violations.

"How much time will I have to correct any problems?"

"We'll be back within 10 days."

"That's very considerate of the inspectors."

Although Bob was being very sarcastic, he figured they didn't get it.

Susie, a kitchen worker, was continually breaking dishes.

She was warned repeatedly until Bob finally deducted money from her pay. When she received her next pay, she talked to Bob.

"Don't ever do that again. I'll report you to the state. You can't make me pay."

"Any more breakage and you'll certainly get a deduction."

During the next few weeks, she broke several big plates. Bob charged her for them. Three weeks later, an inspector from the state appeared at Days.
"Susie Johnson has complained about being charged for broken dishes. Is that correct?"

"Yes, she was very careless and it started to cost me money."

"That's against the state law. Have you ever charged any other employees?"

"Yes, over a period of years."

"You must go over your payroll book and add up all that has been collected. Take 6% and add that to the total. In addition, we intend to assess a steep fine to prevent it from happening again."

Adding 6%, with a big fine together, cost Days $400.00.

During the 1970's the most out-standing group to take over the Auditorium for a three day encampment was the Salvation Army. They represented the Eastern District of 13 states.

Cars and buses brought thousands of Salvationists for their meetings. On the first day they held many preliminary programs at the Auditorium, Tabernacle, Community Room and Thomley Chapel.

During the afternoon the Salvation Army Band put on a great program in Auditorium Square. All throughout the day, enthusiasm built up until evening when everyone headed for the Auditorium.

General Eva Barrows, who headed the Salvation Army throughout the world, was the featured speaker.

Representatives from each of the 13 Eastern states had the flag bearers march down the main aisle and present a gift to the General. It was very impressive sight as the colors were presented.

General Barrows gave an inspirational speech. Directly behind her were the new officers of the Army who would be inducted later.

During the second day various competitions were held with different musical groups and many other meetings were held.

At night a production was presented on the stage. It featured the "Blood of the Lamb." As a person narrated, many skits were shown showcasing the work of the Army.

One spotlighted the homeless. Others provided settings for alcoholics; those overwhelmed with a drinking problem; individuals with marital concerns; persons with physical disabilities; homeless people; and those who lacked clothing, food or decent housing.

As each skit was finished the individuals were led to meet with a Salvationist who helped to solve whatever matters arose out of conflicting social values or relationships. Finally, the individuals made commitments to the Salvation Army.

For the last act, General Booth, the founder of the Salvation Army, was featured.

He was portrayed as being inducted into Heaven.

All the new officers were commissioned and received an assignment to a Salvation Army unit wherever there was need for help.

On Sunday the encampment closed with a grand parade of all units.

Bob, who had attended all the meetings he could, was very impressed with the three days devoted to spiritual needs. He was very challenged with the doctrine as set forth by the Army and wrote out some of its pertinent provisions.
Salvationists believe in only one God; Specify a belief in the God Head-Father, Son and Holy Ghost; accept God's wrath for failure to obey Him; Understand Jesus atoned for all sins; Need for repentance for salvation; Believe in grace provided by faith in Jesus; that believers are kept blameless until Christ returns; Resurrection of the Body and that the wicked shall have endless punishment.

As the years passed, Bob, instead of taking it easy, continued to work long hours. By 1978, he was often working 20 hours a day.

In the third week in August he started at 4 a.m. and never finished until 12:30 a.m. Being completely exhausted, he actually crawled up the stairs. Reaching the top, he entered one of the spare rooms. After throwing off all his clothing, he collapsed on the floor.

The room was pitch black, with no lights on anywhere. His conscience started to work overtime. He remembered how he was hazed with the air hose; overcame the scleroderma on his leg and how lucky his Air Force Group had been with one of Hitler's buzz bombs while in England.

Out of nowhere a thought struck him. He might have been born blind and would never have seen a beautiful sunrise or sunset.

However, he had been given a strong warning to slow down. Naturally, he proceeded to ignore it and finished out the rest of the season. You have to understand his background. Part German with a smattering of Scotch and Irish makes for an almost lethal combination.

Starting out 1979 with a bang, he had a slight relapse around the Fourth of July. Continuing to overwork, he finally had another collapse the last week in August. Bob decided he had been acting stupid too long. So after some discussion with Maisie, Bob decided to list Days with a realtor. ·

One week after advertising the proposed sale, a couple from North Jersey submitted an offer, which was accepted. After several months the sale was completed with several conditions.

A very large mortgage was provided at 8% interest. Maisie and Bob were to remain at Days until March 1st 1980. This arrangement benefited both the seller and the buyer.

The new owners came to Days every week-end and worked on Saturday and Sunday.

In the meantime, Bob purchased a 3-story property at 92 Main Avenue. A great amount of work was needed to get a certificate of occupancy. First a new electric system was installed. Many holes in the walls throughout the house had to be puttied.

Next, the rooms had to be repainted to cover up the hideous color scheme that the previous owner had used. The living room and dining area were sanded and varnished.

Finally, all work was completed and Maisie, Dennis, and Bob prepared for a new start in life. It was time to start really living. Days was history.

Chapter Twelve

Epilogue

Early in the 1970's, Bob became very concerned with the problems of the Ocean Grove Camp Meeting Association. Finally, he decided to write down his impressions.

The final result was a three page typewritten letter, which was sent to all the 26 Trustees.

In the missile, he listed many issues that could have been improved. First and foremost he stated that they had one of the worst public relations he had ever encountered.

Letters with suggestions were often ignored. Regulations were often changed. Programs for Saturday nights in the Great Auditorium were often mediocre with low attendance in many cases. Volunteers were often taken for granted. Repair of streets and sewer system were slighted.

Only two Trustees answered the letter. One man wrote and

said he agreed with Bob. The other gentleman disagreed and said he would talk to Bob in July. He never did.

One year later a local trustee told Bob he would put him up for nomination to the Board.

However, Bob told him not to do so. Result, he received one vote.

Next year, against Bob's advice, he was again nominated. Result-4 votes.

Finally; in the third year, Bob was again nominated. It resulted in eight favorable votes.

Bob finally convinced his trustee friend to stop nominating him. It was an embarrassment to both of them.

After a few months Bob made a decision. For the rest of his life he dedicated himself to helping the Camp Meeting Association and all the citizens of Ocean Grove.

Bob's next book "Journey of Faith", Book II, will focus on what he tried to accomplish in his final years.